THE

RUSSIAN
REVOLUTION

Edited by

Robert V. Daniels

PRENTICE-HALL, INC.
Englewood Cliffs, New Jersey

Library of Congress Cataloging in Publication Data

DANIELS, ROBERT VINCENT, COMP.
    The Russian Revolution. Englewood Cliffs, Prentice-
Hall, [1972]
    (A Spectrum book)
    Bibliography: p.
    1. Russia—History—Revolution, 1917–1921—Sources.
I. Title.
DK265.A5167   947.084′1   72–3958
ISBN 0–13–784801–3
ISBN 0–13–784793–9 (pbk.)

Printed in the United States of America

10   9   8   7   6   5   4   3   2   1

PRENTICE-HALL INTERNATIONAL, INC. (*London*)
PRENTICE-HALL OF AUSTRALIA, PTY. LTD. (*Sydney*)
PRENTICE-HALL OF CANADA, LTD. (*Toronto*)
PRENTICE-HALL OF INDIA PRIVATE LIMITED (*New Delhi*)
PRENTICE-HALL OF JAPAN, INC. (*Tokyo*)

CONTENTS

54723

IV. THE BOLSHEVIKS PREPARE

V. THE OCTOBER UPRISING

VI. THE CONSOLIDATION OF SOVIET POWER

FOREWORD

As the twentieth century draws towards its close, its inhabitants can begin to exercise perspective on its history. When we try to do so, we cannot help but conclude that the great Russian Revolution of 1917–1918 was perhaps the century's most important single historical event. Yet once we have said that, we have said very little. The Russian Revolution was not a single event but a myriad of events. And it had antecedents and causes stretching back into the past, and effects and consequences that are with us still in the 1970s.

In this book, Professor Daniels has focused his attention on the crowded and tumultuous days of the revolutionary upheaval itself. In a succinct introduction he leads us up to the moment of crisis. From then on, with only the commentary needed to orient us, he lets participants and eyewitnesses speak for themselves. Here are the Tsarist secret police warning in October 1916 of the growing unrest, the American Ambassador reporting the first outbreaks in February 1917, the earliest official proclamations of the Provisional Government and of the Soviet of Workers' and Soldiers' Deputies, and the Tsar's own abdication. Then come the clear signs of disciplinary decay in the army, and Lenin's early pronouncements.

A vivid series of documents illustrates the crisis that prevailed between February and October, and we meet and come to know Prince Lvov, Kerensky, Kornilov, and other actors in the drama great and small. We study the Bolsheviks' organizational efforts within the army as described by one of themselves, and live breathlessly through the July Days, when they almost succeeded in overthrowing the Provisional Government. And we watch in turn the deterioration of economic life, the food crisis, the intensifying of discontent among industrial workers, the disintegration of the army as an active fighting force, and the drive for independence among Ukrainians and Finns.

An authoritative contemporary report shows us how critically important were the efforts—and the failure—of the Provisional Government to bring about land reform and satisfy the peasants' yearnings before open revolution in the countryside became ungovernable.

With the ripening of the revolutionary situation in the autumn of 1917, we see Lenin preparing to reap the harvest, and we read his own words in the second half of September calling for immediate action. Despite much hesitation among his followers, his daring insistence won the day, as we can see from the original reports that take us into the inner councils of the Bolsheviks. With the formation of the Military-Revolutionary Committee on October 20, the way was clear, and the last act began. Whether we listen to Lenin's bodyguard quoting Lenin's conversation with a woman streetcar conductor, or to a Bolshevik commissar remembering the preparations for the attack on the Winter Palace, we are hearing authentic voices telling us exactly how it was. We end with the forcible dissolution by Lenin of the one democratically elected assembly in all Russian history, which the Bolsheviks would not allow to function because they had won only 25 percent of the seats.

Some of these selections have never before been translated into English, and are presented in Professor Daniels's own version. To an extraordinary degree they give us a front seat in the theatre of the Russian Revolution, and enable us to see and hear and understand more than was possible for any single human being who actually lived through it.

Robert Lee Wolff
Coolidge Professor of History
Harvard University

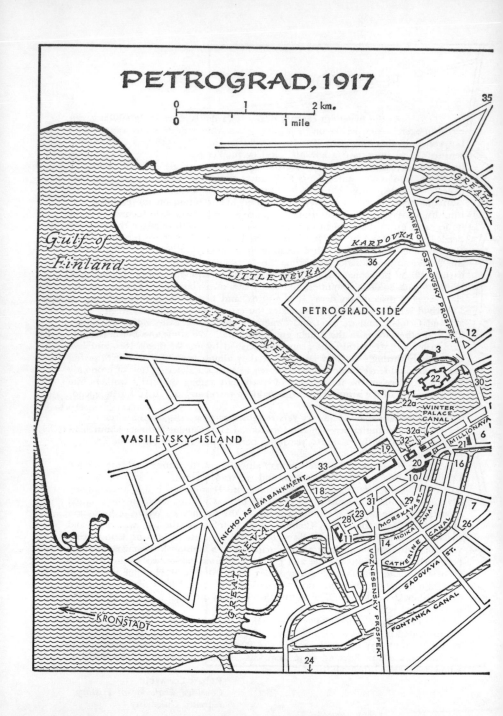

PETROGRAD, 1917

Gulf of Finland

KARPOVKA

LITTLE NEVKA

LITTLE NEVA

PETROGRAD SIDE

KAMENO OSTROVSKY PROSPEKT

GREAT

36

12

3

22

22a

WINTER PALACE CANAL

30

32a

32

MILLIONAYA

21

6

VASILEVSKY ISLAND

19

20

16

NICHOLAS EMBANKMENT

NEVA

33

18

31

37

29

MORSKAYA ST.

10

MOIKA

7

CATHERINE CANAL

28 23

11

14

7

26

SADOVAYA ST.

VOZNESENSKY PROSPEKT

FONTANKA CANAL

GREAT

KRONSTADT

24

35

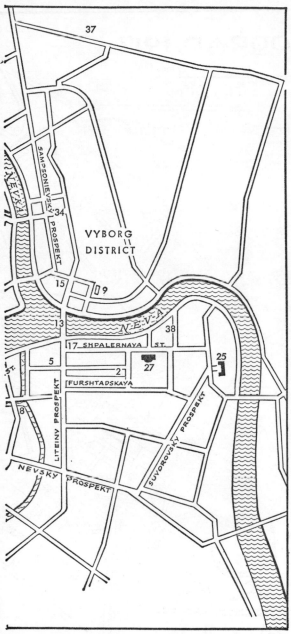

Introduction

The focus of this volume is the wave of revolutionary events in Russia that led from the fall of Tsar Nicholas II to the consolidation of power by the Communists less than a year later. To be sure, the Russian Revolution can be dated over a much longer span than 1917–18. The Old Regime began to crumble as early as the Revolution of 1905, while the revolutionary work of the Communists went on long after the Soviet regime was established, at least to the end of War Communism in 1921. Some would say that the Russian Revolution has not yet ended. However, for the purpose of a brief but in-depth documentary introduction to the historical significance of the Russian Revolution, the period from February, 1917, to January, 1918, is the decisive one, and the limits of this book have been set accordingly.

Revolution as it developed in Russia during these months is a historical phenomenon of a special sort. Great social revolutions, as distinguished from coups d'état, are events in a class by themselves: not only is power violently transferred from one group to another but the whole structure of authority breaks down for a period of time, the entire population is involved in political turmoil, and the basic fabric of society is torn and reshaped for generations to come.

A social revolution of this type is not a momentary event, but rather a process, necessarily working itself out over a period of years. It typically starts with the assumption of power by moderates, and only later manifests its extremist potential. A series of coups d'état may punctuate the progression from moderate to extremist revolutionary politics, and back to a consolidation of the new order.

A social revolution is a highly atypical historical experience in terms of the involvement of the mass of the population in political conflict. The masses for once do make history, or at least set the directions and conditions within which the leaders of the various revolutionary factions may try to make history. In the circumstances of revolution, once the old authority has broken down, all the potential of pent-up frustrations and grievances is actualized. Chaotic and violent group strife becomes the norm.

Characteristically a social revolution is a time of fundamental breakdown in a society's overall system of authority. In fact, it is this breakdown of authority that allows a social revolution to take place. Chaos and conflict will then inevitably deepen until the old authority is reconstructed or a new one is built by whatever contending group proves itself tough and ruthless enough to do the job. This element is not likely to be the democratic idealists who preside over the early stages of a revolution. It will be extremists, since only people willing to use extreme methods will be able to accomplish the job of restoring order. Whether it will be extremists of the Left, fighting for a new world, or extremists of the Right, battling to restore what they represent as the old order, will depend on the specifics of time and place. There remains in the ultimate resolution of the revolutionary upheaval a substantial role for leadership and action, as well as for sheer accident, in deciding which way the process will go at the end.

The stormclouds of revolution had been gathering over Russia for decades before the deluge finally broke in 1917. More self-conscious revolutionary theorizing, plotting, and organizing preceded the Russian Revolution than any other in history. Marxism took root in Russia only after the military conspirators of the "Decembrist" movement in the 1820's, the student "Nihilists" of the 1860's, and the "Populists" and terrorists of the 1870's and '80's had vainly striven to enlist the masses in the cause of revolutionary change.

Real popular support for the revolutionary movement came only with the acceleration of industrialization in Russia in the 1880's and 1890's, and the consequent growth of a mass of unhappy urban workers as well as a more commercialized and politically more aware peasantry. In 1898 a small group of Marxist intellectuals organized the Russian Social-Democratic Workers Party ("SD's"), aspiring to lead the proletariat, and in 1900 the Populists organized the Socialist Revolutionary Party ("SR's") with a largely peasant base. Simultaneously with these developments came the belated appearance of a constitutionalist movement among the middle class and the more enlightened gentry, aspiring to democratic liberties with a minimum of violence. These elements took political form in the Constitutional Democratic Party ("Kadets," from its Russian initials), organized in 1905.

In the face of economic transformation and social ferment, the Russian government under Emperors Alexander III and Nicholas II set itself adamantly against any diminution of the principle of autocracy. Here was the classic pre-revolutionary circumstance, as

the irresistible force of social and economic change collided with
the immovable object of institutional rigidity. It remained only for
Russia's defeat at the hands of Japan in the war of 1904–5 to set the
stage for a near-revolutionary collapse of the government during
the wave of strikes and uprisings known as the Revolution of 1905.

The events of 1905 compelled the regime of Nicholas II to concede
a measure of constitutional government and individual freedom,
with the establishment of the Duma, a parliamentary body of limited power and unequal representation. The liberals attempted to
work within this framework, while the SDs and SRs strove as largely
illegal movements to keep the spirit of revolution alive. Meanwhile
both these socialist parties split on tactical lines: the SRs spawned
an extremist wing dedicated to terrorism, and the SDs divided into
Mensheviks and Bolsheviks over the issue of a democratic or conspiratorial organization. By 1912 the Bolshevik faction of SDs had
become to all intents and purposes a separate party, virtually the
personal creation of its leader Vladimir Ilyich Ulyanov, better
known to history as Lenin.

Some historians argue that the post-1905 regime in Russia, given
a chance to develop undisturbed, might have evolved gradually
into a western-style constitutional democracy, but such a chance
was not to be enjoyed. The fatal stress for the Tsarist system was
the First World War, bringing anguishing losses and economic
privations, and exposing the incompetence of the upper levels of
the government, which was plagued with reactionary intrigues cen-
tering around the Empress Alexandra and the infamous faith-healer
Rasputin. The war spelled an abrupt reversal of the progress Russia
had been enjoying, a downturn corresponding to the so-called "J-
curve" phenomenon in many immediately pre-revolutionary situations. By 1917 the government was almost universally hated, though
the proximity and ease of its collapse were scarcely dreamed of in
any quarter.

The Russian Revolution had all the characteristics of breakdown
and social strife that distinguish the great social revolution. It
opened with a spectacular instance of the spontaneous collapse of
an old authority, when the throne of Nicholas II was toppled by
rioting workers and mutinous troops in the capital city of Petrograd.
Overthrow of a traditional monarchy characterizes practically all
great revolutions, but in Russia this event came relatively early, at
the very outset (unless the beginning of the revolutionary process
is dated from 1905).

The fall of the Tsar opened the way for a typically moderate, well-meaning but socially limited and ineffectual regime, the Provisional Government headed by Prince Georgi Lvov. Even the representatives of the potentially most radical social forces—the leaders of the Petrograd Soviet—initially voiced a spirit of moderation. None of this benevolent atmosphere, however, could survive the profound breakdown of authority and discipline throughout the social system that commenced with the disappearance of the tsarist police state. Russia plunged into an orgy of democracy—in the factories, in the army, in the villages, no less than in the organs of local government where the ad hoc representative rule of the soviets (complete with the instantaneous recall of deputies who fell out of step with the masses) was in many places a reality well before the Bolshevik insurrection.

Truly Russia met the standard of a social revolution in the way the masses were galvanized and mobilized into direct and violent political involvement. Grievances and hopes unchained by the moderate revolution crystallized with lightning speed—the peasants' hunger for land, the workers' urge to control the factories, the national minorities' longing for self-determination—while the moderate Provisional Government, headed after July by the vaguely socialist lawyer Alexander Kerensky, postponed the resolution of these urges in the hopes of quieter and more legal solutions later on. Hanging over it all was the issue of the war against Germany and the Central Powers, a fatal complication of the Russian Revolution. The masses would not go on fighting, certainly not for the goals of imperial expansion, while the Provisional Government hesitated to betray its allies. Meanwhile the soldiers in growing numbers rebelled against traditional military discipline and authority as well as against the idea of more pointless combat. More than any other issue it was the war which paralyzed the Provisional Government and destroyed any possibility of peaceful evolution in Russia.

As Russian society sank deeper into chaos and disorder with each passing month, candidates for the restoration of effective authority spoke more and more insistently. Essentially there were two alternatives: either the right wing business and military leadership, rallying around the Chief of Staff General Kornilov, or the Bolshevik Party of Lenin. Kornilov saw his chance in August, 1917, and attempted by a show of force either to coerce or to overthrow the Kerensky government. (It never became quite clear which was his intention.) The outcome of this bid from the Right was a total failure, only playing into the hands of the extreme Left. Meanwhile, the characteristic social processes of revolution, with the radicalization of wider and wider groups of the population, were daily adding to the strength of the Bolsheviks, the only political group (along with their allies of the Left Socialist Revolutionary Party) ready to acknowledge the most extreme demands of the masses.

For the Bolsheviks, riding on the crest of the revolutionary wave, it remained only to translate their potential into the actual seizure of power. This proved to be more complicated than the abstract conception of history as forces and agents would suggest. Lenin, framing a program of violent insurrection, met with varying degrees of resistance from his own supporters, who wanted to hedge against failure or dress their anticipated victory in some degree of democratic procedure. When the October Revolution finally came, it was the product of an extraordinarily complicated interplay among the Kerensky government, Kerensky's left and right wing opposition within the government, and the divided and improvising Bolshevik leadership. As is more often than not the case, historical necessity may have posed the alternatives, but contingency decided among them.

The violence in which the Soviet regime was born was only the first in a series of cataclysmic events through which the political and social institutions of the Soviet Union were eventually forged, including Civil War, terror, and foreign intervention; the retreat and consolidation of the New Economic Policy in the 1920's; the renewed revolutionary drive under Stalin with collectivization and the Five-Year Plans; and finally Stalin's purges. There is no altogether clear stopping-place for a historical narrative, and certainly not in the saga of the Russian Revolution. However, the events of January, 1918 do serve as a logical point to close an account focusing on the revolutions of 1917. The dispersal of the only representative body that Russia ever elected in a genuinely democratic fashion signalled the basic consolidation of Bolshevik (or Communist, as the party was restyled in March, 1918) rule through the soviets and the commitment to one-party dictatorship that has distinguished the Soviet regime ever since.

This collection of source materials is focused especially on the events surrounding the Bolshevik takeover, not only because of the intrinsic importance of the event—for the outside world no less than for Russia—but also to afford the reader some opportunity, close-up and in detail, to observe how history actually happens in a critical episode. All too often the student is left with an impression of events as a generalized blur. From the compressed and abstract narrative of a text he has little chance to experience either the way in which events actually took place or the manner in which the historian apprehends and reconstructs those events from the documentary record. It is hoped that the materials on the background and accomplishment of the Bolshevik Revolution presented here will serve as a useful example of history in the raw, even though they are necessarily selective and abridged.

One of the facts of life about the primary materials of history is the limitation in quality or adequacy of the documents themselves, with the attendant pitfalls in trying to reconstruct history from an incomplete record. The Bolshevik Revolution is a particularly humbling example of this elusiveness of history. The sources are often contradictory; eyewitnesses make mistakes and even state as fact events which never occurred; later historians and governments twist or suppress accounts; key documents are missing. Nowhere is there a document of the Bolshevik plan of revolution; nowhere (except for John Reed's unsubstantiated recollection) is there a record of any Bolshevik decision to start the uprising. The question one must therefore face is whether the revolution was in fact deliberately planned and launched, as everyone on all sides naturally assumed afterwards.

All this is only to illustrate the point that direct confrontation and struggle with the messy documents themselves is the only way in which a student can appreciate what history actually is. At the same time this approach is bound to make the study of history more meaningful and exciting, as a closeup of the nature of life in human society, and as a sample of the genuine process of inquiry into human affairs.

The study of Russian materials involves certain technical problems which may be clarified here. Until February, 1918, Russia was officially on the Julian calendar, thirteen days behind the Gregorian calendar of the West. Hence February 27, 1917, "old style," was March 12 in the West, "new style"; and October 25 in Russia was November 7. In this book old style dates are used throughout to conform to contemporary terminology. The capital of Russia until 1918, originally St. Petersburg, was called by its Russian form, Petrograd, after 1914, and later (in 1924) renamed Leningrad; here again the contemporary form, Petrograd, is followed. The Russian slang name "Piter" is translated "St. Pete."

The spelling of Russian terms and names in the roman alphabet has never been entirely standardized. Where the usage of particular names has become more or less standard it is followed; otherwise the Library of Congress system without diacritical marks is used. Occasionally spellings employed in older translations have been amended to conform to these rules.

Sources of the respective documents and of the translations are indicated in the introduction to each item.

I am grateful to Professor Robert Lee Wolff for his many helpful comments and criticisms, to Elaine Luthy for a meticulous job of editing, and to Carolyn Perry and Barbara Huston for their labors in preparing the typescript. I am indebted to The National Endowment for The Humanities and The Harvard Russian Research Center for a year's fellowship support to study the process of revolution, during which time the present work was brought to completion.

Part One

THE FALL OF THE TSAR

The February revolution was a truly spontaneous event, surprising the enemies of the old regime as much as the Emperor himself, although the underlying tensions in wartime Russia were perfectly obvious in the police report which begins this selection of documents. The responses to the event documented in the subsequent selections were hasty improvisations on all sides—with the possible exception of the concluding item of this chapter, Lenin's greetings to Russia on his return from exile.

Causes of the Revolution: An Inside View

It is generally acknowledged that the precipitating cause of the Russian Revolution was the First World War and the unmanageable burden which it placed on Russia's inflexible political and economic system. The conditions brought on by the war were recorded nowhere as graphically as in a secret and hence frank and uncensored (however turgid) report by the secret police in Petrograd in October, 1916.

The document was published by the Soviet authorities in 1926 under the title, "The Political Situation in Russia on the Eve of the February Revolution as Spotlighted by the Police," in *Krasny Arkhiv* (The Red Archive), no. 16. (Excerpts from pp. 4–7 and 24; editor's translation.)

*Report of the Petrograd Okhrana Division to the
Special Branch of the Department of Police. October, 1916. Top Secret*

The exceptional seriousness of the historical situation
which the country is experiencing, those innumerable catastrophic
hardships which may threaten the whole vital basis of the state, the
imminently possible rebellious manifestations among the lower orders of the population of the empire, who are by conviction loyal
elements but are exasperated by the burdens of everyday existence
—all this compellingly dictates the urgent necessity of quick and
exhaustive measures to eliminate the present confusion and to dissi-
pate the excessively heavy atmosphere of social dissatisfaction. . . .
The brilliant results of the offensive of the armies of General
Brusilov in the spring of the current year 1916 and the simultaneous
state of affairs in the supply of the battle front definitely show that
the tasks assumed by the government and broad circles of society
in the said direction have been fulfilled more than successfully. The
question of furnishing the armies with military supplies can be considered answered and settled in the proper manner. But on the
other hand, the constantly worsening disorganization of the rear,
in other words of the whole country, manifesting a chronic and
more and more progressive character, has at the present time at-
tained such a maximum and monstrous development that it is
definitely now beginning to threaten the results that have been
achieved on the battle front, and promises in the shortest time to
throw the country into the ruinous chaos of catastrophic and elemental anarchy.
The systematically growing disruption of transportation; the un-
restrained bacchanal of free-booting and robberies by a novel kind
of shady operators in various branches of the commercial, industrial
and social-political life of the country; the unsystematic and
mutually contradictory assignment of representatives of the governmental and local administration; the lack of conscientiousness on
the part of the secondary and lower agents of authority in the
provinces, and, as a consequence of all the foregoing, the unequal
distribution of food supplies and items of prime necessity, the

incredibly rising cost of living and the absence of sources and means of feeding the presently starving population of the capitals [Petrograd and Moscow] and the major social centers . . . ; all this, taken together, characterizing in bright, comprehensive colors the result of neglect of the rear, as the basic source and cause of the serious sick condition of the internal life of the vast state organism, at the same time definitely and categorically indicates that a terrible crisis is already ripe and must necessarily be decided in one direction or the other.

Characteristic confirmation of the above can be supplied by the especially disturbed mood now observed among the mass of the population. At the beginning of September of this year among the widest and most diverse strata of the inhabitants of the capital there was abruptly noticed an exceptional rise in opposition activity and ugliness of mood. More and more often complaints began to resound about the administration, expressing sharp and merciless condemnation of the policy of the government.

Towards the end of said month this mood of opposition, according to the data of extremely well-informed sources, reached such exceptional proportions as had never before been present among the broad masses even in the period 1905–1906. Openly and without restraint lamentations began to resound about the "venality" of administration, the incredible burdens of the war, the unbearable conditions of everyday existence; cries of radical and leftist elements about the need "first of all to destroy the internal German[1] and then take care of the outside one" began to meet a more and more sympathetic attitude in relation to them.

The serious material situation of the rank-and-file citizen, doomed to a half-starving existence and not seeing any ray of light in the immediate future, makes him turn sympathetically and with unusual attention to any sort of plans and projects that are based on promises to improve the material conditions of life. As a result, circumstances have arisen that are favorable in the highest degree to any sort of revolutionary propaganda and enterprises, and that have been quite correctly appraised by the active leaders of the leftist and other anti-government groups; it is hard to deny as well the possibility of the work, concealed by these favorable circumstances, of secret German agents, who have for some time been repeatedly proclaiming to the whole world that Russia is on the eve of revolution, that armed uprising is more than imminent in

---

[1] [A reference to alleged pro-German sympathies in the imperial court—Ed.]

Petrograd, to the end of achieving the speedy conclusion of peace, etc.

Undoubtedly rumors like this are significantly exaggerated in comparison with the true state of affairs, but nevertheless the situation is so serious that attention must necessarily be given to it without delay. The Kadet circles of the capital,[2] extremely well acquainted with the economic situation of the citizen, long ago predicted that Russia was near, if not to revolution, then in any case to severe disorders, capable of breaking out everywhere if the appropriate preventative measures were not taken.

In the recent period, in a series of various committees caring for refugees, in the food supply commissions, in city welfare offices and other diverse institutions coming into close contact with the citizen, with his needs and his mood—all without exception express a definite conviction that "we are on the eve of big events," in comparison with which "1905 was child's play"; that the system of government holding the citizen in ignorance has suffered a complete collapse: The citizen has waked up and instead of the expected "hurrah" is crying "help," etc. . . .

Summing up the foregoing views of all the main Russian political parties, which to a notable degree vividly characterize the mood of diverse circles of the population of the country—even on condition of allowing in these views for a certain element of "tendentiousness" and blowing-up—it is necessary to recognize as unconditional and indisputable, that the internal set-up of Russian governmental life at the present time finds itself under the severe threat of immediately impending serious shocks, brought on and explained exclusively by economic motivations: hunger, unequal distribution of food supplies and objects of prime necessity, and the fantastically rising cost of living. Questions of food supply in the broadest circles of the population of this vast empire are the single arousing impulse that is driving these masses gradually into association with the growing movement of dissatisfaction and exasperation. In the present instance there are definite and precise data making it possible to assert categorically that for the time being this whole movement has a strictly economic foundation and is connected with hardly any purely political programs. But it is only necessary for this movement to be cast in some concrete form and to be expressed in some definite act (a pogrom, a major strike, a massive clash of the lower orders of the population with the police,

---

[2] [I.e., The Constitutional Democratic ("Kadet") Party—ED.]

etc.), and it will at once and unconditionally become purely political. . . .

The February Revolution

Late in February, 1917, food riots and strikes snowballed
into open mass defiance of the government, almost exactly according to the scenario anticipated in the warnings by the police. On the 26th of February military units were ordered to fire
on unruly crowds. Then the decisive turn came: the troops refused to shoot, turned against their officers, and by joining
the protest movement turned it into a revolution. By noon on
the 27th, the authority of the Russian monarchy had ceased
to exist.

There are a multitude of eyewitness accounts of the February events, but one of the most graphic is contained in a dispatch sent back to Washington by the American Ambassador,
David R. Francis (Dispatch no. 632 to the Secretary of State,
February 27/March 12, 1917; U.S. National Archives, file
861.00/331).

On Friday, March 9th,[1] crowds visited a number of factories and ordered the men to stop work, which was promptly done.
Yesterday, Sunday, there were soldiers in the streets and perhaps 50
people were killed or wounded, but most of the firing was with
blank cartridges. Yesterday evening the order was given that no
persons should go on the streets to-day and no vehicles would be
allowed. About ten A.M. today a regiment of 1000 to 1200 men stationed in barracks about two blocks from the Embassy mutinied
and according to reports killed their commanding officer because
he would not join them.

At 11:30 A.M., Mr. Miles phoned me from the Second Division in
the Austrian Embassy [under U.S. care prior to American entry into
the war] that some of the mutineers accompanied by many revolutionists had visited the munition factory adjoining the Austrian
Embassy; had killed the officer in command there, and had ordered
the men to quit work; that many of the employees had come into
the Austrian Embassy, and one lieutenant, in order to conceal

----

[1] [February 24, old style—ED.]

themselves from the angry crowd. Mr. Miles said that he had and was at the time he phoned endeavoring to prevent more employees from entering the Embassy but fearing that the crowd might learn that the Embassy was being used as a refuge he called me up and requested that an additional guard should be requested immediately. I phoned to the Foreign Office and was assured that the guard would be strengthened if possible, but it must be done by the War Department or General Staff, with which the Foreign Office would immediately communicate by phone. That was the last communication I have had with the Foreign Office and this dispatch is written at 8 P.M. For four or five hours past there have been crowds on the Liteiny which is the most frequented thoroughfare in this section of the city and Secretary Bailey who came into the Embassy from his apartment at about 3:30 P.M. reported that he had seen four dead men lying on Liteiny and there were also five wounded men. Within one hour thereafter many of the mutineers were seen walking on Furshtatdskaya in front of the Embassy, some with guns and some without, and there marched by the Embassy in the roadway a body of about one hundred men in citizens' clothes who carried muskets but observed no order of marching and appeared to have no commanding officer. During this hour, from 4 to 5 P.M. there also passed in front of the Embassy a number of motor cars filled with soldiers with guns, but in every car there were some citizens or men in citizens' clothes who were no doubt revolutionists. About this hour the Embassy was informed by telephone that the Duma had been dissolved or prorogued until about the middle of April— I heard later that this order was issued yesterday afternoon but as there have been no newspapers for two days past it was not known until the hour for the Duma's assemblage, and I suppose the members were ignorant of it until they went to the hall of the meeting. At about six o'clock P.M., Captain McCully, the Naval Attaché of the Embassy, who had left for his apartment about 5 P.M., phoned that in his walk from the Embassy to his apartment, a distance of over a mile, he had seen no policemen nor any soldiers who acknowledged fealty to the Government but he had observed a thousand or more cavalrymen riding quietly toward the [river] Neva and abandoning the streets of the city to the mutineers and revolutionists. About 6:30 P.M. the telephone connection of the Embassy was severed but whether by the Central Office or by the revolutionists is not known. Between 7:30 and this writing, 9:30 P.M., many rumors have come to the Embassy through the Secretaries and other attachés. Mr. Basil Miles, Director of the Second Division, took the women employees from the Austrian Embassy to the Hotel de France, where they are quartered for the night. Mr. W. F. Sands, Asst. Director, is sleeping in the Austrian Embassy tonight. The city seems entirely quiet but absolutely under the control of the soldiers who have mutinied, and of the revolutionists. It is reported that six regiments have joined the revolutionists and the Government seems to have abandoned all effort to curb the revolution. One rumor is to the effect that the Duma, after being dissolved, assembled notwithstanding the royal decree, and declared the Ministry deposed and made the President of the Duma, Rodzianko, the President of the Council of Ministers. The President of the Imperial Council [Prince N. D. Golitsin], a Reactionary, is said to be under arrest. Another rumor is to the effect that Grand Duke Nicholas has been made Commander-in-Chief of all the Russian forces to supplant the Emperor [Nicholas II]. I cannot vouch for the truth of any of these rumors, but the Duma has certainly been prorogued until the middle of April, and the order to that effect is said to have been signed by the Emperor several days ago.

I had telephonic talk with Moscow today about noon and Consul-General Summers reported that everything was quiet in that city; the treatment of the Duma, however, will arouse every section of the Empire. No one can fortell what tomorrow will bring forth. It is said that the Ministers of State have all left their respective houses for fear the revolutionists will arrest them. One theory is that the city has been abandoned and will be subjugated by being starved out.

Everything depends upon the Army. If the Grand Duke Nicholas, who is known to be very antgaonistic to Pro-German influences, which are said to be dominating the Emperor through the Empress, should assume command of the Army it would be very likely to rally to his appeal. The Emperor, however, has many friends, and it is not likely that he will yield without a struggle.

The antagonism to the Minister of the Interior, Protopopov, is bitter and quite general as he is charged with being the creature of Rasputin and is also suspected of German sympathy and of having assisted in bringing about the scarcity of food in order that the resulting unrest might justify Russia in making a separate peace.

The Formation of the Provisional Government

A "temporary committee" of members of the Duma, having defied the Tsar's order to dissolve, undertook to maintain order in Petrograd and to work for a constitutional monarchy. Prodded by the simultaneous organization of the Petrograd Soviet, the temporary committee announced the assumption of executive power by a new cabinet on March 2, and proclaimed its aims to the people of Russia on March 6.

The following proclamations were originally published in *Izvestia* ["*The News*"], March 3, 1917, and the *Bulletin of the Provisional Government*, March 7, 1917. The English translations are from Frank A. Golder, ed., *Documents of Russian History, 1914–1917* (New York: The Century Co., 1927), pp. 308–9, 311–13. This and all following selections from this volume are reprinted by permission of Appleton-Century-Crofts, Educational Division, Meredith Corporation.

Citizens, the Provisional Executive Committee of the members of the Duma, with the aid and support of the garrison of the capital and its inhabitants, has triumphed over the dark forces of the Old Regime to such an extent as to enable it to organize a more stable executive power. With this idea in mind, the Provisional Committee has appointed as ministers of the first Cabinet representing the public, men whose past political and public life assures them the confidence of the country.

PRINCE GEORGE E. LVOV, Prime Minister and Minister of the Interior

P. N. MILIUKOV, Minister of Foreign Affairs

A. I. GUCHKOV, Minister of War and Marine

M. I. TERESHCHENKO, Minister of Finance

A. A. MANUILOV, Minister of Education

A. I. SHINGAREV, Minister of Agriculture

N. V. NEKRASOV, Minister of Transportation

A. I. KONOVALOV, Minister of Commerce and Industry

A. F. KERENSKY, Minister of Justice

VL. LVOV, Holy Synod [Church Affairs]

The Cabinet will be guided in its actions by the following principles:

1. An immediate general amnesty for all political and religious offenses, including terrorist acts, military revolts, agrarian offenses, etc.

2. Freedom of speech and press; freedom to form labor unions and to strike. These political liberties should be extended to the army in so far as war conditions permit.

3. The abolition of all social, religious and national restrictions.

4. Immediate preparation for the calling of a Constituent Assembly, elected by universal and secret vote, which shall determine the form of government and draw up the Constitution for the country.

5. In place of the police, to organize a national militia with elective officers, and subject to the local self-governing body.

6. Elections to be carried out on the basis of universal, direct, equal, and secret suffrage.

7. The troops that have taken part in the revolutionary movement shall not be disarmed or removed from Petrograd.

8. On duty and in war service, strict military discipline should be maintained, but when off duty, soldiers should have the same public rights as are enjoyed by other citizens.

The Provisional Government wishes to add that it has no intention of taking advantage of the existence of war conditions to delay the realization of the above-mentioned measures of reform.

> President of the Duma, M. RODZIANKO
> President of the Council of Ministers, PRINCE LVOV
> Ministers MILIUKOV, NEKRASOV, MANUILOV, KONOVALOV,
> TERESHCENKO, VL. LVOV, SHINGAREV, KERENSKY.

Citizens of Russia:

A great event has taken place. By the mighty assault of the Russian people, the old order has been overthrown. A new, free Russia is born. The great revolution crowns long years of struggle. By the act of October 17 [30], 1905, under the pressure of the awakened popular forces, Russia was promised constitutional liberties. Those promises, however, were not kept. The First State Duma, interpreter of the nation's hopes, was dissolved. The Second Duma suffered the same fate, and the Government, powerless to crush the national will, decided, by the act of June 3 [16], 1907, to deprive the people of a part of those rights of participation in legislative work which had been granted.

In the course of nine long years, there were taken from the people, step by step, all the rights that they had won. Once more the country was plunged into an abyss of arbitrariness and despotism. All attempts to bring the Government to its senses proved futile, and the titanic world struggle, into which the country was dragged by the enemy, found the Government in a state of moral decay, alienated from the people, indifferent to the fate of our native land, and steeped in the infamy of corruption. Neither the heroic efforts of the army, staggering under the crushing burdens of internal chaos, nor the appeals of the popular representatives, who had united in the face of the national peril, were able to lead the former Emperor and his Government into the path of unity with the people. And when Russia, owing to the illegal and fatal actions of her rulers, was confronted with gravest disasters, the nation was obliged to take the power into its own hands.

The unanimous revolutionary enthusiasm of the people, fully conscious of the gravity of the moment, and the determination of the State Duma, have created the Provisional Government, which considers it to be its sacred and responsible duty to fulfil the hopes of the nation, and lead the country out onto the bright path of free civic organization.

The Government trusts that the spirit of lofty patriotism, manifested during the struggle of the people against the old regime, will also inspire our valiant soldiers on the field of battle. For its own part, the Government will make every effort to provide our army with everything necessary to bring the war to a victorious end.

The Government will sacredly observe the alliances which bind us to other powers, and will unswervingly carry out the agreements entered into by the Allies. While taking measures to defend the country against the foreign enemy, the Government will, at the same time, consider it to be its primary duty to make possible the expression of the popular will as regards the form of government, and will convoke the Constituent Assembly within the shortest time possible, on the basis of universal, direct, equal, and secret suffrage, also guaranteeing participation in the elections to the gallant defenders of our native land, who are now shedding their blood on the fields of battle.

The Constituent Assembly will issue the fundamental laws, guaranteeing to the country the inalienable rights of justice, equality, and liberty. Conscious of the heavy burden which the country suffers because of the lack of civic rights, which lack stands in the way of its free, creative power at this time of violent national commotion, the Provisional Government deems it necessary, at once, before the convocation of the Constituent Assembly, to provide the country with laws for the safeguarding of civic liberty and equality, in order to enable all citizens freely to apply their spiritual forces to creative work for the benefit of the country. The Government will also undertake the enactment of legal provisions to assure to all citizens, on the basis of universal suffrage, an equal share in the election of local governments.

At this moment of national liberation, the whole country remembers with reverent gratitude those who, in the struggle for their political and religious convictions, fell victims to the vindictive old regime, and the Provisional Government will regard it as its joyful duty to bring back from their exile, with full honors, all those who have suffered for the good of the country.

In fulfilling these tasks, the Provisional Government is animated by the belief that it will thus execute the will of the people, and that the whole nation will support it in its honest efforts to insure the happiness of Russia. This belief inspires it with courage. Only in the common effort of the entire nation and the Provisional Government can it see a pledge of triumph of the new order.

The Soviet of Workers' and Soldiers' Deputies

Reviving the tradition of the St. Petersburg Soviet ("council") of 1905, the leaders of the various socialist parties convened the Petrograd Soviet of Workers' and Soldiers' Deputies on the very day of the revolution, February 27. This body, elected by the factories and military units, immediately acquired much more authority in the eyes of the masses than the nominal Provisional Government, though it chose to give its support to the latter for the time being.

The documents following are the initial proclamation of the Soviet, published in *Izvestia* on February 28, 1917, and the Soviet's resolution of March 7 on relations with the Provisional Government. The English translations are from Golder, pp. 287–88, 310–11.

To the People of Petrograd and Russia from the Soviet of Workers' Deputies

The old regime has brought the country to ruin and the population to famine. It was impossible to bear this longer, and the inhabitants of Petrograd came out on the street to express their dissatisfaction. They were greeted by a volley of bullets. In place of bread, the Tsar's Ministers gave them lead.

But the soldiers would not act against the people and turned against the Government. Together with the people they seized guns, arsenals, and important governmental institutions.

The fight is still on and must go on to the end. The old power must be completely crushed to make way for popular government. In that lies the salvation of Russia.

In order to succeed in this struggle for democracy, the people must create their own governmental organ. Yesterday, February 27, there was formed at the capital a Soviet of Workers' Deputies, made up of representatives of factories, mills, revolted troops, and democratic and socialistic parties and groups. The Soviet, sitting in the Duma [building], has set for itself as its main task to organize the popular forces, and to fight for the consolidation of political freedom and popular government.

The Soviet has appointed commissars to establish the people's authority in the wards of Petrograd. We invite the entire population of the capital to rally at once to the Soviet, to organize local committees in their wards and take into their hands the management of local affairs.

All together, with our forces united, we will fight to wipe out completely the old Government and to call a constituent assembly on the basis of universal, equal, direct, and secret suffrage.

Resolution Adopted by the Soviet, March 7

First.—Pursuant to the decision of the Soviet of Workers'
and Soldiers' Deputies, and in conformity with the general policy
laid down by the same, the Executive Committee of the Soviet of
Workers' and Soldiers' Deputies finds it necessary to adopt immediate measures to keep the Soviet informed regarding the intentions
and acts of the Government; to keep the latter, in turn, informed
regarding the demands of the revolutionary people; to exert influence upon the Government for the purpose of satisfying these
demands; and to exercise constant control over its actions.

Second.—To carry out this resolution, the Executive Committee
of the Soviet of Workers' and Soldiers' Deputies elects a delegation
composed of the following comrades: Skobelev, Steklov, Sukhanov,
Filipovsky, and Chkheidze; and instructs them to enter at once
into negotations with the Provisional Government.

Third.—After the result of these negotiations becomes known,
a delegation shall be elected for the establishment of permanent relations with the Council of Ministers, as well as with individual
ministers and government departments, for the purpose of carrying
into effect the demands of the revolutionary people.

The Abdication of Nicholas II

The Revolution found Tsar Nicholas at Army Headquarters in Mogilev, whence he vainly tried to get back to the capital by train, while the Duma Committee was preparing to
depose him in favor of his son. Confronted by the Duma emis-
saries in the town of Pskov, Nicholas agreed to abdicate, but
in favor of his brother, who in turn declined the throne and
allowed it to lapse.

Nicholas' abdication manifesto was originally published in
the "Izvestia of the Committee of Petrograd Journalists,"
March 3, 1917. The English translation is from Golder, pp.
297–98.

In the midst of the great struggle against a foreign foe, who has been striving for three years to enslave our country, it has pleased God to lay on Russia a new and painful trial. Newly arisen popular disturbances in the interior imperil the successful continuation of the stubborn fight. The fate of Russia, the honor of our heroic army, the welfare of our people, the entire future of our dear land, call for the prosecution of the conflict, regardless of the sacrifices, to a triumphant end. The cruel foe is making his last effort and the hour is near when our brave army, together with our glorious Allies, will crush him.

In these decisive days in the life of Russia, we deem it our duty to do what we can to help our people to draw together and unite all their forces for the speedier attainment of victory. For this reason we, in agreement with the State Duma, think it best to abdicate the throne of the Russian State and to lay down the Supreme Power.

Not wishing to be separated from our beloved son, we hand down our inheritance to our brother, Grand Duke Michael Alexandrovich, and give him our blessing on mounting the throne of the Russian Empire.

We enjoin our brother to govern in union and harmony with the representatives of the people on such principles as they shall see fit to establish. He should bind himself to do so by an oath in the name of our beloved country.

We call on all faithful sons of the Fatherland to fulfil their sacred obligations to their country by obeying the Tsar at this hour of national distress, and to help him and the representatives of the people to take Russia out of the position in which she finds herself, and to lead her into the path of victory, well-being, and glory.

May the Lord God help Russia!

NICHOLAS

March 2, 1917, 3 P.M.
City of Pskov.

Countersigned by the
Minister of the Imperial Court,
Adjutant-General, Count Fredericks.

Order Number One

The spirit of democratic revolution was nowhere more graphically illustrated than in the so-called "Order Number One" drafted and issued by a crowd of soldiers with Bolshevik help at the Soviet building on March 1. The impact was to proclaim democracy in the army and cripple the military authority of the Provisional Government.

The order was published in *Izvestia*, March 2, 1917. The English translation is from Golder, pp. 386–87.

March 1, 1917

To the garrison of the Petrograd District, to all the soldiers of the guard, army, artillery, and navy, for immediate and strict execution, and to the workers of Petrograd for their information:—

The Soviet of Workers' and Soldiers' Deputies has resolved:

1. In all companies, battalions, regiments, parks, batteries, squadrons, in the special services of the various military administrations, and on the vessels of the navy, committees from the elected representatives of the lower ranks of the above-mentioned military units shall be chosen immediately.

2. In all those military units which have not yet chosen their representatives to the Soviet of Workers' Deputies, one representative from each company shall be selected, to report with written credentials at the building of the State Duma by ten o'clock on the morning of the second of this March.

3. In all its political actions, the military branch is subordinated to the Soviet of Workers' and Soldiers' Deputies and to its own committees.

4. The orders of the military commission of the State Duma shall be executed only in such cases as do not conflict with the orders and resolutions of the Soviet of Workers' and Soldiers' Deputies.

5. All kinds of arms, such as rifles, machine guns, armored automobiles, and others, must be kept at the disposal and under the control of the company and battalion committees, and in no case be turned over to officers, even at their demand.

6. In the ranks and during their performance of the duties of the

service, soldiers must observe the strictest military discipline, but outside the service and the ranks, in their political, general civic, and private life, soldiers cannot in any way be deprived of those rights which all citizens enjoy. In particular, standing at attention and compulsory saluting, when not on duty, is abolished.

7. Also, the addressing of the officers with the title, "Your Excellency," "Your Honor," etc., is abolished, and these titles are replaced by the address of "Mister General," "Mister Colonel," etc. Rudeness towards soldiers of any rank, and, especially, addressing them as "Thou," [1] is prohibited, and soldiers are required to bring to the attention of the company committees every infraction of this rule, as well as all misunderstandings occurring between officers and privates.

The present order is to be read to all companies, battalions, regiments, ships' crews, batteries, and other combatant and noncombatant commands.

Lenin Calls for a New Revolution

The new freedom of revolutionary Russia permitted thousand of revolutionary leaders to return from jail, Siberia, or foreign exile. Lenin arrived from Switzerland on April 3 and immediately shocked not only the moderates but even his own followers with his "April Theses," calling for a new proletarian revolution to overthrow the Provisional Government.

This document was originally published in the Bolshevik paper *Pravda* [The truth] on April 7, 1917. English translation from V. I. Lenin, *Selected Works* (Moscow: Foreign Languages Publishing House, 1951), vol. 2, part 1, pp. 13–17.

Theses

1. In our attitude towards the war, which also under the new government of Lvov and Co. unquestionably remains on Rus-

---

[1] [Russian "ty," the second person familiar pronoun—ED.]

sia's part a predatory imperialist war owing to the capitalist nature of that government, not the slightest concession to "revolutionary defensism" is permissible.

The class-conscious proletariat can give its consent to a revolutionary war, which would really justify revolutionary defensism, only on condition: a) that the power pass to the proletariat and the poorest sections of the peasantry bordering on the proletariat; b) that all annexations be renounced in actual fact and not in word; c) that a complete break be effected in actual fact with all capitalist interests.

In view of the undoubted honesty of the broad strata of the mass believers in revolutionary defensism, who accept the war as a necessity only, and not as a means of conquest, in view of the fact that they are being deceived by the bourgeoisie, it is necessary with particular thoroughness, persistence and patience to explain their error to them, to explain the inseparable connection existing between capital and the imperialist war, and to prove that without overthrowing capital *it is impossible* to end the war by a truly democratic peace, a peace not imposed by violence.

The most widespread propaganda of this view in the army on active service must be organized.

Fraternization.

2. The specific feature of the present situation in Russia is that it represents a *transition* from the first stage of the revolution—which, owing to the insufficient class consciousness and organization of the proletariat, placed the power in the hands of the bourgeoisie —*to the second* stage, which must place the power in the hands of the proletariat and the poorest strata of the peasantry.

This transition is characterized, on the one hand, by a maximum of legally recognized rights (Russia is *now* the freest of all the belligerent countries in the world); on the other, by the absence of violence in relation to the masses, and, finally, by the unreasoning confidence of the masses in the government of capitalists, the worst enemies of peace and Socialism.

This peculiar situation demands of us an ability to adapt ourselves to the *special* conditions of Party work among unprecedentedly large masses of proletarians who have just awakened to political life.

3. No support for the Provisional Government; the utter falsity of all its promises should be explained, particularly those relating

to the renunciation of annexations. Exposure in place of the impermissible illusion-breeding "demand" that *this* government, a government of capitalists, should *cease* to be an imperialist government.

4. Recognition of the fact that in most of the Soviets of Workers' Deputies our Party is in a minority, and so far in a small minority, as against *a bloc of all* the petty-bourgeois opportunist elements, who have yielded to the influence of the bourgeoisie and convey its influence to the proletariat, from the Popular Socialists and the Socialist-Revolutionaries down to the Organization Committee (Chkheidze, Tsereteli, etc.), Steklov, etc., etc.

It must be explained to the masses that the Soviets of Workers' Deputies are the *only possible* form of the revolutionary government, and that therefore our task is, as long as *this* government yields to the influence of the bourgeoisie, to present a patient, systematic, and persistent *explanation* of the errors of their tactics, an explanation especially adapted to the practical needs of the masses.

As long as we are in the minority we carry on the work of criticizing and exposing errors and at the same time we preach the necessity of transferring the entire power of state to the Soviets of Workers' Deputies, so that the masses may by experience overcome their mistakes.

5. Not a parliamentary republic—to return to a parliamentary republic from the Soviets of Workers' Deputies would be a retrograde step—but a republic of Soviets of Workers', Agricultural Labourers' and Peasants' Deputies throughout the country, from top to bottom.

Abolition of the police, the army and the bureaucracy (i.e., the standing army to be replaced by the arming of the whole people).

The salaries of all officials, all of whom are to be elected and to be subject to recall at any time, not to exceed the average wage of a competent worker.

6. In the agrarian program the most important part to be assigned to the Soviets of Agricultural Labourers' Deputies.

Confiscation of all landed estates.

Nationalization of *all* lands in the country, the disposal of the land to be put in the charge of the local Soviets of Agricultural Labourers' and Peasants' Deputies. The organization of separate Soviets of Deputies of Poorest Peasants. The creation of model farms on each of the large estates (varying from 100 to 300 desiatins,[1] in accordance with local and other conditions, by decisions of the local institutions) under the control of the Soviets of Agricultural Labourers' Deputies and for the public account.

7. The immediate amalgamation of all banks in the country into a single national bank, and the institution of control over it by the Soviets of Workers' Deputies.

8. It isn't our *immediate* task to "introduce" Socialism, but only to bring social production and distribution of products at once under the *control* of the Soviets of Workers' Deputies.

9. Party tasks:
a) Immediate convocation of a Party congress;
b) Alteration of the Party program, mainly:
  1) On the question of imperialism and the imperialist war;
  2) On our attitude towards the state and *our* demand for a "commune state" (i.e., a state of which the Paris Commune [the short-lived revolt of 1871] was the prototype);
  3) Amendment of our antiquated minimum program.
c) Change of the Party's name.[2]

10. A new International.
We must take the initiative in creating a revolutionary international, an International against the *social-chauvinists* and against the "Centre."

[1] [One desiatina = approx. 2.7 acres—Ed.]
[2] Instead of "Social-Democracy," whose official leaders *throughout* the world have betrayed Socialism and deserted to the bourgeoisie (the "defensists" and the vacillating "Kautskyites"), we must call ourselves a *Communist Party*. [Lenin's note.]

Part Two
🎨 THE PROVISIONAL GOVERNMENT IN CRISIS

The revolutionary honeymoon of the Provisional Government and the Soviet was short-lived. It was the issue of the war —whether to prosecute it or to end it, and on what terms—that drove the first sharp wedges into the ranks of the well-meaning moderate revolutionaries, and created the pattern of political disunity and instability that plagued the Provisional Government throughout its short life. By summer, as the social dynamics of revolution were intensifying, more uncompromising challenges to the Provisional Government appeared on both the Left and the Right. Although the government was momentarily successful in dealing with these threats, its social foundations were being cut away on both sides, leaving it by the fall of 1917 in an impossibly precarious position.

The April Crisis

The first serious tremors for the Provisioial Government came scarcely six weeks after it had taken office, when Foreign Minister Paul Miliukov's efforts to reassure Russia's allies about the war provoked armed demonstrations in the streets and led to a cabinet crisis. Miliukov and War Minister Alexander Guchkov were forced to resign, making way for a coalition cabinet including several representatives from the Soviet. Kerensky moved from the Justice Ministry to become Minister of War.

Miliukov recounted the crisis, with emphasis on the role Kerensky allegedly played in engineering his own ouster, in

his *Political Memoirs, 1905–1917,* ed. Arthur P. Mendel, trans.
Carl Goldberg (Ann Arbor, Michigan: The University of Michigan Press, 1967), pp. 445–46, 448–54. Copyright © 1967 by
the University of Michigan Press; reprinted by permission of
the publisher.

When Lenin began delivering his criminal speeches before tremendous crowds from the balcony of Ksheshinskaya's home,[1]
I insisted in the government on his immediate arrest. Alas, the
Provisional Government did not decide to do this.

With the arrival of the Russian Zimmerwaldists,[2] the pressure of
their views on the Soviet was strongly increased. Agitation was
carried over into worker and soldier circles, and extreme demands
were presented to the Soviet in the name of factories, plants, sections of the garrison, post and telegraph workers, and so on. They
put forward the same slogan I had refused to allow in the appeal
to the citizens on March 28: The Soviet was to demand that the
government send an address to the Allies without delay, proposing
that they, in turn, renounce "annexations and indemnities." Only
by this increased pressure can we explain, obviously, Kerensky's
speech to the English socialists, his false report about the note
supposedly being prepared, and, finally, the raising of the question
of such a note in the government itself. A new campaign was begun
against me, but this time on a broader front. It was obviously impossible to refuse all concessions, but I chose a path which still
defended myself and my policy.

I consented to send our allies a note, not demanding anything
from them, but informing them of our views on the aims of the
war which had already been expressed in the address to the citizens
on March 28. The government agreed to be satisfied with this. We
had only to think up a pretext for this declaration to the Allies and
to compose the accompanying note. The note was to serve as a
subject for discussion in the government. My pretext consisted of
refuting the rumors that Russia was preparing to conclude a separate peace with the Germans. I refuted them by saying that "the
general principles already expressed by the Provisional Government
(in the appeal of March 28) correspond completely to those high
ideals—concerning the liberating character of the war, the creation

---

[1] [The mansion of a former mistress of the Tsar, taken over by the Bolsheviks
to serve as party headquarters—ED.]
[2] [Anti-war socialists including Lenin and the Bolsheviks; from the name of
the town in Switzerland where they conferred in 1915—ED.]

of a stable foundation for the peaceful co-existence of peoples, the self-determination of the oppressed nationalities—ideals which have been constantly expressed by many leading statesmen in the Allied countries," especially America [which had just entered the war]. Such ideas, I continued, could be expressed only by a liberated Russia, a Russia capable of "speaking the language that can be understood by the advanced democracies of contemporary humanity." Such statements not only gave no reason to think of a "weakening of Russia's role in the common, Allied struggle" but, on the contrary, they strengthened "the national aspirations of carrying the world war to a decisive finish"; the general attention here was focused on "the task which is immediate and urgent for everyone: to repulse the enemy who has invaded the very borders of our homeland." I then repeated Kokoshkin's [a Kadet jurist] insertion: "The Provisional Government, defending the rights of our homeland, will fully observe the obligations which it has accepted regarding our allies, as was said in the reported document." In conclusion, the note repeated, first of all, confidence in a "victorious finish to the present war in total agreement with our allies," and, in the second place, our assurance that "the questions raised by this war will be solved in the spirit of creating a solid foundation for a lasting peace, and that the advanced democracies, inspired by identical aspirations, will find the means to obtain those guarantees and sanctions necessary for the prevention of new bloody conflicts in the future." The words "guarantees and sanctions" were inserted by me at the insistent request of Albert Thomas [the French Socialist representative], who, evidently, still did not want to throw away his Allied "ballast." These words were dangerous if they were understood, for example, in the sense of guarantees and sanctions for France from Germany upon conclusion of peace. However, they did secure me the French socialists' consent to my note.

On April 18, my note was ready and approved by the government; the following day the Soviet was informed of it. April 18 corresponded to May 1 New Style, and the Soviet prepared to celebrate the workers' holiday. The main celebration was held in Mars Field. Beginning in the morning, from all corners of the capital, processions of workers, soldiers, and others streamed to the field with placards and red banners. From my ministerial offices, I had the pleasure of seeing the inscription on the roof of the Winter Palace in huge letters: "Long Live the International." Included among the placards were such as "Down with the war," while a resolution of the factory workers had still earlier demanded the resignation of the Provisional Government and the transfer of power into the hands of the Soviet. These Bolshevik demonstrations, however, were drowned in the general character of the holiday: the Soviet printed in *Izvestia*, that "they do not correspond to the views of the Soviet." The processions were well organized, and passed by in perfect order. The numerous speeches given by street orators, and the general mood of the crowd regarded the Leninists disapprovingly. Albert Thomas was delighted with the grandeur of the celebration and exclaimed: "What beauty, what beauty!" Here was a Soviet holiday. . . .

On . . . May 3 (N.S.) [April 20, Old Style] the Bolsheviks took their revenge for the peaceful Soviet holiday of May 1. My note was published on that day, and it served as an excuse for the first armed demonstration in the streets of the capital against me and against the Provisional Government. By 3 or 4 o'clock in the afternoon, a reserve battalion of the Finnish Regiment marched to the Marinsky Palace with placards reading: "Down with Miliukov," "Miliukov, resign." Behind them came companies from the 180th Reserve Battalion and about one company from the Baltic naval depot. The majority of the soldiers did not know why they were being led. In a letter on April 23 (O.S.) to *Novaya Zhizn* [New life], Fedor Linda, a member of the Soviet, admitted that he was "responsible." In addition to the troops, adolescent workers also took part in the demonstration without hiding the fact that they were each paid ten to fifteen rubles for doing so. The leaders of the Soviet could no longer be blamed, because the Soviet, limiting itself to applying "pressure," was in no way planning to take the place of the government. Indeed, the Soviet found itself in an embarrassing position, somewhere between my note and the Bolsheviks. . . .

. . . On April 21, the Bolsheviks attempted an armed struggle. From the workers' quarters to Mars Field, disciplined columns of workers marched behind detachments of Red Guards with placards "Down with War!" and "Down with the Provisional Government!" By evening there was shooting on the streets and victims fell. . . .

It was Prince Lvov's lot to bring up the question of the ministerial crisis, and he did so at the same meeting with the Executive Committee, on April 21, which was discussed above. As far as I remember, the question took me by surprise, since I was not yet aware of the talks which were going on behind my back. Moreover, Prince Lvov introduced his proposal, as was his habit, in an indecisive and optional form. Of course, unlike Kerensky, he was not planning to make use of the crisis for himself personally, and one could argue with him only on grounds of principle—which, indeed, I had the occasion to do in the next few days.

In the April 21 session, Prince Lvov began right off with the statement: "The aggravated situation which has come about as the result of the note of April 18 is only a private affair. During the recent weeks, the government has generally been placed under suspicion. Not only does it find no support among the democratic masses, but it even meets with attempts to undermine its authority. In such a situation the government does not consider that it has the right to bear the responsibility. We (I exclude myself from this "we"—P.M.) decided to invite you here and talk the matter over. We should know whether or not we are fit for our responsible post at the given time. If not, then, for the good of the homeland, we are ready to lay down our authority and give our places to others." . . .

. . . Prince Lvov personally was not planning to resign; rather, he planned to remain at the head of a "coalition." We have already seen Kerensky's intentions [to gain power]. The transition to a coalition with the socialists was supposed to return the confidence of the "revolutionary democratic masses" to the government and to create an excuse for changing the government's composition. Prince Lvov's practical suggestion was formulated in this latter sense: "to renew efforts directed at broadening the composition of the government."

I resolutely protested against publishing this accusatory-apologetic act and against bringing socialists into the government. I showed that the government would only discredit itself by admitting its failures and that the introduction of socialists would weaken governmental authority. Both of my protests were completely futile. In the spirit of Prince Lvov, the appeal itself acknowledged, on the one hand, that the government found its support, not "in coercion and force, but in the voluntary obedience of free citizens" and, on the other hand, that the "impossibility" of overcoming the difficulties of its tasks was due to the fact that the government refused to use "the old violent methods of rule and the external, artificial means of raising the prestige of the governing authorities." This was very idealistic, but far too Tolstoyan. The appeal recognized that "among the less educated and less organized strata of the population," "violent and anarchic acts" were occurring in the country, which threatened "to bring the country to disintegration at home and defeat at the front." Nevertheless, the appeal did not indicate any measures to prevent those results except to say that the path "of civil war and anarchy, bringing disaster to liberty, should not be the path of the Russian people . . . the path from liberty to the return of despotism is well known in history."

At the session of April 21, I learned that my own personal fate had already been decided, once and for all. V. Chernov, Kerensky's dangerous rival in the [Socialist Revolutionary] party and the destined candidate for the post of minister of agriculture, declared "with his usual banal grimaces, his sugary smile and affectations" (in Nabokov's[3] words), that "both he and his friends have unlimited respect for P. N. Miliukov, that they consider his participation in the Provisional Government necessary, but that, in their opinion, Miliukov could better develop his talents at any other post, even as Minister of Education." . . .

Guchkov's resignation forced the Executive Committee of the Soviet to reconsider its decision [not to enter the cabinet]. On the evening of May 1 (O.S.), it was decided by a majority of 41 to 18 that the socialists would join a coalition government—with a definite program. Included here were "annexations and indemnities"[4] and controversial points of social and agrarian policy; the paragraph on the army, however, proclaimed the "strengthening of the fighting force at the front"—apparently in view of Kerensky's obligations to the Allies to inspire the army with revolutionary enthusiasm. We hurried back from Headquarters, and beginning on the morning of May 2, I took part in the discussion of the Soviet's declaration. Similar declarations in addition to our objections were introduced by the People's Freedom party and the Temporary Committee of the State Duma. Together we demanded, above all, the formal recognition of the new government as the only organ of power. The Kadets then demanded recognition of the government's exclusive right to use force and command the army. In social, national, and constitutional questions, the Kadet party demanded that the government not anticipate the decisions of the Constituent Assembly. In the event that its demands were not satisfied, the party, acting on Kerensky's own principle, reserved for itself the right to recall its members from the government. This was all published in greater detail in the party's declaration of May 6—simultaneously with the government's declaration which made a few, but entirely unsatisfactory, concessions to us. Thus, the "coalition" from the very beginning was based, not on a full agreement, but on a rotten

---

[3] [V. D. Nabokov, a Kadet leader and father of the novelist—ED.]

[4] [I.e., the Soviet's demand for "a democratic peace without annexations and indemnities."—ED.]

compromise which carried the struggle between the Soviet and the government right into the new cabinet. As before, I continued to protest against the very principle of a coalition, and it was on this question of principle, and not only on the question of the future conduct of our foreign policy, that I based my resignation. A typical scene followed when, upon leaving the session, I went around the table shaking the hands of my colleagues who remained. When I came to Prince Lvov, he grabbed hold of my hand, and holding it in his own, incoherently babbled: "But what do you mean? What is this? No, don't go; but, no, you will come back to us." I coldly tossed him the phrase: "You were warned"—and walked out of the room.

Kerensky and the Offensive

On becoming Minister of War, Kerensky undertook the goal of restoring the fighting capacity of the army and demonstrating Russia's power to her allies. To this end, he broke the relative quiet of the Eastern Front by ordering an offensive against the Austrians, initially successful but rudely reversed in July by a German counter-offensive.

Kerensky explained his reasoning in his memoirs, *The Catastrophe: Kerensky's Own Story of the Russian Revolution* (New York and London: D. Appleton & Co., 1927), pp. 184–85, 189, 207–9, 222–24. (Copyright © 1927 by D. Appleton & Co.; reprinted by permission of Hawthorn Books, Inc. and O. A. Kerensky.)

In reply to the question of Prince Lvov as to whom, among the civilians available, the high command would recommend for the War Ministry, General Alexeyev replied: "The first candidate of the high command is Kerensky."

The task placed upon me as War Minister by the Provisional Government was in brief this: restoration by all means at hand of the fighting capacity of the army. To accomplish this I was to move the army to an offensive, sparing no efforts.

Of course my task would have been quite impossible if at that time, in the middle of May, there had not appeared in the masses the marked evidences of the deep psychological change produced by the Stokhod experience [a local German offensive]. The resolutions of various Soviets, army committees and the declarations of delegations arriving in Petrograd from the front, all spoke of but one thing: the imperative need of restoring the fighting capacity of the army and the productive capacity of the workers, as essential prerequisites to the defense of the country. . . .

On assuming my duties at the War Ministry, I first of all issued an order to the sulking members of the commanding corps forbidding the resignation of any officers of the army in the field. This measure nipped in the bud the intention of certain high commanders to resign by way of protest against the official publication of the "Declaration of the Rights of Soldiers." I believed that discipline was to be demanded first from people who by virtue of their position should have served as models of the performance of duty. Moreover, it was quite impossible to stop publication of the notorious declaration, first, because it had already long been published by the *Izvestia* of the Petrograd Soviet, and second, because Polivanov and Guchkov had made the official and categorical promise to the Soviet and army committees that the declaration would be put into effect, stating that the delay in doing so was due entirely to causes of a technical nature.

After putting a stop to the sulking attitude of the generals, I immediately published the "Declaration of the Rights of Soldiers." But, under my revision of it, the declaration received an interpretation which prompted Lenin, in the *Pravda*, to term it the "Declaration of the Lack of Rights of Soldiers" and to begin a mad campaign against the new war minister. The fourteenth point of the declaration, excluded originally by General Polivanov, on the demand of the Soviet, but restored by me, declared:

"At times of action the commander has the right to apply any measures, including the use of armed force, against subordinates who fail to obey his orders."

This point was the first move towards restoration of the power and authority of commanders. But even the most courageous officers did not for a long time venture to use this power. In addition to this fundamental change, the eighteenth point of the revised declaration placed the right of appointment and removal exclusively in the hands of commanders, and omitted the clause of the Polivanov original which vested the army committees with the right of recommendation and rejection of appointees. Thus I did away with the right of subordinates to participate in the appointment of their superiors. . . .

At first glance my "conservatism," coming upon the "radicalism" of Guchkov, may appear paradoxical. As a representative of the Left, the normal procedure would have been for me to pursue a radical policy. But what may appear abnormal under normal conditions, becomes in the abnormal revolutionary situation but a normal development of events. My entrance into the War Ministry marked the end of the period of destruction and the beginning of the period of construction, not only in the army, but in the country as a whole.

All my initial measures were undertaken merely with the object of clearing the field for my basic activity, the bringing about of a sharp change in the attitude and sentiment of the army. This required my presence at the front and not in Petrograd. From the first day of my appointment as Minister of War and up to my assumption of the premiership, after the first Bolshevist uprising, July sixteenth to twentieth [3rd to 7th, O.S.], I spent the greater part of my time on various parts of the front, taking no part, on my brief returns to Petrograd, in the work of the Provisional Government so far as internal matters were concerned. . . .

We no longer find to-day the unanimity of opinion concerning our offensive of July, 1917, that prevailed then both in Russia and among the Allies. Due apparently to a misconception, some even consider that offensive as the last blow that killed the Russian army. Others believe that the operation was determined not by the interests of Russia but was "dictated" to us by our Allies. A third group is inclined to see in it a particular manifestation of "light-headedness" and irresponsibility on the part of the government in having permitted itself to be carried away by love of rhetoric.

The last opinion deserves no reply. The fact is that the resumption of active operations by the Russian army after two months of paralysis was dictated absolutely by the inner development of events in Russia. To be sure, the representatives of the Allies insisted on the execution by Russia, at least in part, of the strategic plan adopted at the Inter-Allied conference in Petrograd, in February, 1917. But the insistence of the Allies would have been of no avail if the necessity for the offensive had not been dictated by our own political considerations. The insistence of the Allies (France and England) played no part, if only because they no longer considered themselves bound by any obligations to Russia after the Revolution. As I have already said, the German General Staff having stopped, according to plan, all active operations on the Russian Front, there ensued a condition of virtual armistice. It was the plan of the German High Command that this armistice be followed by a separate peace and the exit of Russia from the War. Berlin's efforts to come to a direct agreement with Russia were begun as early as April. Of course, these efforts failed to make any impression on the Provisional Government and the whole Russian democracy, which were determined on peace as quickly as possible, but a general, not a separate peace. . . .

It was not possible to rely upon a new blow from Germany that would definitely bring the Russian democracy, dreaming of peace, to the realization of the bitter facts of the situation. It was necessary to make a choice—to accept the consequences of the virtual demobilization of the Russian army and capitulate to Germany, or to assume the initiative in military operations. Having rejected the idea of a separate peace, which is always a misfortune for the country concluding it, the return to a new action became unavoidable. For no army can remain in indefinite idleness. An army may not always be in a position to fight, but the expectancy, at all times, of impending action constitutes the fundamental condition of its existence. To say to an army in the midst of war that under no circumstances would it be compelled to fight is tantamount to transforming the troops into a meaningless mob, useless, restless, irritable and, therefore capable of all sorts of excesses. For this reason and to preserve the interior of the country from the grave wave of anarchy threatening from the front it was incumbent upon us, before embarking upon the main problem of army reorganization and systematic reduction and readjustment of its regular formations, to make of it once more an army, *i.e.*, to bring it back to the psychology of action, or of impending action. . . .

On the first day of the battle we captured 10,000 prisoners and several cannon, but failed to break through the line towards Brjezany. Indecisive also were the battles on our right flank, where the eleventh army was in action. Guns, prisoners, but not a step forward!

There where last year Brusilov attacked the Austrian Slavs were now only German and Hungarian divisions, with an admixture of Turks.

But on the left flank, where the eighth army was in action, our troops in a few days achieved a brilliant success. After breaking through the Austrian Front at Kalush, the troops of General Kornilov and General Cheremisov broke through deep into the enemy lines, capturing, on July tenth, the old city of Galich.

The success at Kalush was facilitated by the fact that on this part of the front there were many Slavs in the enemy's ranks. In addition, our command had succeeded in obtaining, a few days before the battle, all the necessary information concerning the disposition of the enemy troops and the plans of the enemy's command.

The offensive of the Russian troops occurred exactly four months after the outbreak of the Revolution, midway between March [February] and November [October].

The operations begun by us in Galicia were later extended to the Western Front commanded by General Denikin and to the Northern Front. Very soon they lost their offensive character and became purely defensive actions. The failures of the Russian armies thereupon became one of the sharpest and most poisonous weapons in the struggle against the Provisional Government conducted by the leaders of the Kornilov military conspiracy, which matured in September [August]. But this utilization for political purposes of the restoration of the fighting capacity of the Russian army cannot, looked at objectively, belittle its historical significance. . . .

After the first moments of military weakening, Russia after the Revolution continued to hold the enemy on her front, in numbers at least equal to the prerevolutionary period. Thanks to the psychological influence exerted by the Russian Revolution on the populations of the Central Empires, to which I have already referred, Ludendorff [the German Chief of Staff] was compelled to concentrate purely German divisions on the Russian Front in numbers yet unprecedented during the entire period of the War.

The strategic task on the Russian Front in the year 1917 was carried out in full: the liquidation of the War through German victory, pending the entrance of the United States into active operations, became impossible.

The Bolshevik Military Organization

Immediately after the February Revolution the Bolsheviks set up a Military Organization of the party, headed by N. I. Podvoisky, to agitate among the troops and turn their frustrations to the advantage of the Bolsheviks. The Military Organization rapidly succeeded in challenging the authority of the Provisional Government among the troops and in laying down the foundations for Bolshevik victory in October.

In August Podvoisky reported on his progress, in his "Report of the Military Organization," Sixth Congress of the RSDWP (Bolsheviks), August, 1917, *Protocols* (Moscow, 1958), pp. 59–64. (Editor's translation.)

Comrades! Our work among the troops of St. Petersburg began the very next day after the overthrow of the autocracy.

The soldiers wanted to get directives from the Soviet, and turned to anyone, but could not get anything. I recall the night of February 27–28 as the beginning of the Military Organization. A delegation organized by Comrade Molotov came from the units, and then fourteen men signed up in the Party organization. In the Tauride Palace there were two members of the Bureau of the [Bolshevik] Central Committee, myself, and some other comrades. We decided to direct the movement among the soldiers coming in for directions into a definite channel, and proposed that they return to their battalions, hold elections for representatives, and demand that the workers' deputies admit soldiers' deputies as well into the Soviet. . . .

As of March 9 regular work among the soldiers began. The Bolshevik section in the Soviet tried to direct the work along the line of struggle against liberal influences.

At the end of March, thanks to the strong pressure of our comrades serving among the troops, a constituent assembly of Social-Democratic soldiers and officers was convoked, and it was decided to set up a permanently functioning apparatus for the regular direction of work of organization and agitation in the army. This apparatus was the Military Organization. An editorial commission was quickly formed under the M.O. for the publication of the newspaper "Soldiers' Pravda."

In view of the fact that few soldiers were attending the workers' meetings, it was decided that our comrades would go among the barracks and there arrange meetings, even if small ones. But this work turned out to be beyond the capability of our young organization, and a new organizational apparatus was developed—the "Pravda" soldiers' club, which at once won great sympathy. Masses of soldiers flocked to the club. The soldiers who belonged to the club began to conduct propaganda in their units, which almost at once was expressed in the strengthening of our position among the troops. Soon the club became the center where comrades returning from the front headed, and where questions of the war and current policy were debated. . . .

Just at this time Comrade Lenin arrived in Russia. The Military Organization was able to mobilize around seven thousand men to meet him. Comrade Lenin, loudly and clearly proclaiming the idea of a Third International, evoked unprecedented anger against himself. The idea of international unification was clearly too far off for most of the soldiers, and a poisonous issue took root [that Lenin was pro-German]. We had to struggle with the results of this slander for about two weeks. We not only utilized our organization and the club, but also summoned about two hundred more agitators from Kronstadt [the nearby naval base], who scattered among the barracks, talked there with the soldiers, and to a significant degree were able to shake the distrust of the Bolsheviks that had appeared in the regiments. Then huge meetings were arranged, and the foul slander was dissipated.

On April 15 the "Soldiers' Pravda" appeared. Prior to its appearance we had found out what significance a soldiers' newspaper could have at the present moment. . . .

After the publication of the paper our work in St. Pete became significantly easier.

On April 18 there were not too many units with us in the demonstration, but all the units who came out marched with our slogans.

On April 20–21, in the days of the crisis, the M.O. was able to bring out in all two regiments.

At the end of April the ferment grew among the troops; April 23 should be considered the date when dissatisfaction appeared among the mass of the soldiers. This was the day when the declaration of the "lack of rights" of the soldiers was issued.[1]

After the declaration was issued a definite urge appeared among the soldiers to go out onto the streets. We received constant demands to set up meetings to clarify the meaning of the declaration, which served as excellent agitational material.

By this time we had around 6000 members in the M.O., and about thirteen battalions (70,000 out of 140,000 men [in Petrograd]) under our influence. At this time the number of delegates from the units reached 321.

In the course of the next two weeks we heard insistent demands from various regiments to arrange a demonstration of protest against Kerensky's policy [of restoring military authority].

A move of the soldiers onto the streets became unavoidable. We

[1] [Refers to the "Declaration of the Rights of the Soldiers," proposed by the moderates in the Soviet at this time, adopted by Kerensky with further restrictions on May 11—ED.]

had to present to the Central Committee quite flatly and point out that leaving the soldiers to themselves at this moment so important to them would mean the loss of our influence on the mass of the soldiers.

Now, it has been alleged that the preparations for the demonstration of June 10 had a "conspiratorial" character. This is altogether untrue. The Central Committee called some meetings with the Petrograd Committee, the Military Organization, representatives of the wards, regiments, and plants, etc. At these gatherings the mood of the units was determined and the question was asked whether the units would go out into the streets if the Congress of Soviets was against the move. The answer was obtained to the effect that there was no possibility of restraining the move.

The demonstration of June 18 showed the full strength of our influence, since almost all the units marched under our banners. . . .

. . . In the middle of June we were able to hold a conference. . . .

(Podvoisky reads the resolution, "On the Objectives and Tasks of the M.O.," adopted at the All-Russian Conference of Front and Rear Military Organizations.)

"1. The Military Organization of the Russian Social-Democratic Workers' Party, as one of the units of the organization of the whole proletariat, puts at the top of the list of basic and principal tasks the same task as any other organization of our party: to wit, the propaganda and dissemination among the soldiers (composed in the mass of poor peasants and workers) of the same principles and ideas of revolutionary socialism and the clarification of the tactical slogans and programmatic demands of revolutionary Social-Democracy.

"2. Considering the specific character of the milieu in which the military organizations have to work, to wit the milieu of poor peasants who constitute the majority of our army, the Military Organization, without departing for a minute from the basis of class struggle, must strive to make out of the Military Organization such an agitational and propaganda center as can serve as a unifying apparatus for the work of Social-Democracy among the broad mass of the peasant democracy and the semi-proletarian elements of the village.

"3. The special conditions in which the Russian Revolution is flowing forth, specifically the circumstances of the World War, place on the Military Organizations in addition the extremely serious obligation to strengthen in an organized way in the active army the ideas of international socialism, to prepare the necessary conditions for successful struggle for the triumph of the world revolution against world capital and the liquidation of the World War by way of revolution.

"4. Finally, the circumstances of the moment we are experiencing within Russia set before the military organizations one more important task. The unfinished character and grand scale of the Russian Revolution and the special role of the Russian Revolution (indicated in point 3) in the world-wide proletarian revolution that is opening as a result of this unprecedented imperialist war, together with the broad prospects of profound radical reform which still remain in the sphere of the land and workers question, present to the military organizations the task of striving to form, out of the revolutionary-democratic elements of the army that are joining and following the Social-Democracy, an armed material bulwark for the revolution and the demands which it has placed on the agenda."

The July Days

Revolutionary emotion grew rapidly among the populace and troops in Petrograd, fanned both by Bolshevik agitation and the Provisional Government's attempts to restore discipline. Violent demonstrations broke out on July 3, and the fate of the government hung in the balance, but the failure of the Bolsheviks to capitalize on the situation with sufficient resolution permitted the leaders of the government and the Soviet to restore order and hand the extremists a severe though temporary setback.

a) The events of the July Days are recounted in the famous eyewitness account by the Menshevik journalist N. N. Sukhanov, *The Russian Revolution, 1917: A Personal Record,* edited, abridged, and translated by Joel Carmichael (London: Oxford University Press, 1955), pp. 429–31, 440–43, 449–50. (Reprinted by permission.)

My recollections of that day [July 3] begin again at about 6 or 7 in the evening. At 7 o'clock a meeting of the Workers'

Section of the Soviet began in the White Hall. The overwhelming majority was Bolshevik. Was this meeting connected with the movement that had begun, and what, in general, was the Bolshevik Party's relation to it? I don't know for certain. According to all the data, the Bolshevik Central Committee did not organize a demonstration for July 3rd—unlike what had happened on June 9th. I know that the temper of the masses was considered somewhat "worse," a little softer, less well-defined, than three weeks before. It was somewhat dejected by the fiasco of the 9th and by the official Soviet demonstration of the 18th. An uprising, of course, was considered inevitable, for the capital was seething and the general situation was unendurable. The Bolsheviks were getting ready for it—technically and politically. But it was clear that they had not scheduled it for July 3rd. And the Bolsheviks in the Soviet, after meeting during the day, agreed to go to the factories and barracks to agitate against the demonstration.

From various outskirts of the city, beginning with the Vyborg Side, masses of workers and soldiers were moving towards the centre. The workers had left their benches in thousands and tens of thousands. The soldiers were coming out armed. Both had banners bearing the slogans that had predominated on the 18th: "Down with the Ten Capitalist Ministers!" "All Power to the Soviets!"

It was reported that some workers' detachments and two regiments, the 1st Machine-Gunners and the Grenadiers, were approaching the Tauride Palace. An enormous agitation began in the hall. The aisles and the seats for the public, empty up to then, as at ordinary sessions, suddenly filled up with people. Kamenev suddenly leaped up on to the speaker's platform. And this indecisive Right Bolshevik was the first to give official sanction to the uprising.

"We never called for a demonstration," he cried out, "but the popular masses themselves have come out into the streets, to show their will. And once the masses have come out our place is with them. Our task now is to give the movement an organized character. The Workers' Section must here and now elect a special body, a Commission of twenty-five people to control the movement. The others should go to their own districts and join their detachments." There was no doubt that Kamenev's resolution would be accepted. Whether on his own initiative or according to instructions received, Kamenev was far from trying to isolate the Bolsheviks as the instigators of the uprising; as always, he acted conciliatorily. But I cannot find in my memory the slightest trace of any activities during the July Days of the newly-elected "Commission." . . .

Meanwhile the movement was already pouring through the city. The tempest was unleashed. Everywhere in the factories the same thing as had been reported by the *Promyot* worker on the 'phone was going on: workers' and soldiers' delegations would turn up, refer to "all the others," and demand in someone's name that they "come out." Only a minority, of course, demonstrated, but everywhere work was abandoned. Trains ceased to leave from the Finland Station. In the barracks short mass-meetings took place, and then from all sides enormous detachments of armed soldiers made their way towards the centre—some of them to the Tauride Palace. Some started shooting into the air: the rifles went off by themselves.

From early evening, lorries and cars began to rush about the city. In them were civilians and soldiers with rifles at the trail and with frightened-fierce faces. Where they came hurtling from and why—no one knew.

The city fairly quickly took on the look of the last days of February. Since then four months of revolution and liberty had passed. The garrison of the capital, and even more the proletariat, were now strongly organized. But the movement appeared to have no more "consciousness," discipline, or order. Elemental forces raged.

One of the insurgent regiments, led by a Bolshevik lieutenant, was moving along the Nevsky, from the Sadovoy towards the Liteiny. It was an imposing armed force. It was probably enough to hold the city—unless it came up against a similar armed force. The head of the regiment had started to turn into the Liteiny, when some shots were heard from Znamensky Square. The commander of the column, who was riding in a car, turned around and saw the heels of the soldiers, running off in all directions. A few seconds later the car was left alone in the middle of a jeering crowd on the Nevsky Prospect. There were no casualties. . . . I was told all this by the commander himself—now a well-known Bolshevik military leader. Something similar was going on at this time at various points of the capital.

The insurgent army didn't know where it should go, or why. It had nothing but a "mood." This wasn't enough. The soldiers led by the Bolsheviks, in spite of the complete absence of any real resistance, showed themselves to be really worthless fighting material. But not only Bolsheviks led the soldiers' groups that "came out" on July 3rd: unquestionably there were also some completely obscure elements present.

The "over-forties" also came out: that day their representatives had again seen Kerensky and again pleaded to be allowed to go home to work on the land. But Kerensky refused: after all, the offensive against the insolent enemy still continued, for the glory of the gallant Allies. So the "over-forties" gladly joined the "uprising" and in enormous numbers for some reason moved on to the Tauride Palace. . . .

The Kronstadters were unquestionably the chief trump of Lenin's party and the decisive factor in his eyes. Having decided the night before [i.e., on July 3] to summon the masses to a "peaceful demonstration," the Bolsheviks were of course taking steps to mobilize Kronstadt. During the hours of nocturnal wavering, when the movement began to die down, Kronstadt became the sole trump of those members of the Bolshevik Central Committee who sponsored the uprising. . . . Then they countermanded the insurrection. But they had evidently not taken the appropriate steps with respect to Kronstadt—or else one Bolshevik hand didn't know what the other was doing. I don't know exactly what the facts were.

But in any case this is what happened: at around 10 o'clock in the morning there came up to the Nicholas Embankment, where there was a tremendous concentration of people, upwards of forty different ships with Kronstadt sailors, soldiers, and workers. According to Lunacharsky some 20,000 of these "peaceful people" had landed. They were armed and their bands came with them. Landing at the Nicholas Embankment, the Kronstadters formed columns and made their way—to Kshesinskaya's house, the Bolshevik headquarters. They evidently had no precise strategic plan, and only quite a vague idea of where to go or just what to do. They were simply in a mood definitely hostile to the Provisional Government and the Soviet majority. But the Kronstadters were led by Roshal and Raskolnikov—and led to Lenin.

Once again the chances of a new revolution had risen extraordinarily high. Lenin must have very much regretted that the summons to the Petersburg proletariat and garrison had been cancelled as a result of his overnight vacillations. At this point it would have been quite possible to lead the movement as far as he liked. And it was also quite possible to bring about the desired overturn, that is, at least to liquidate the Capitalist Ministers, and the Socialist Ministers and their Mamelukes into the bargain.

In any case Lenin must have begun wavering again. And when the Kronstadters surrounded Kshesinskaya's house, expecting to receive instructions, Lenin made an extremely ambiguous speech from the balcony. He didn't demand any concrete action from the impressive force standing in front of him; he didn't even call on his audience to continue the street demonstrations—even though that audience had just proved its readiness for battle by the troublesome journey from Kronstadt to Petersburg. Lenin merely agitated strongly against the Provisional Government and against the Social-traitors of the Soviet, and called for the defence of the revolution and for loyalty to the Bolsheviks.

According to Lunacharsky, he, Lunacharsky, had been passing Kshesinskaya's house at exactly that time. During the ovation given Lenin by the Kronstadters, Lenin called him over and suggested that he speak to the crowd. Lunacharsky, always ablaze with eloquence, didn't wait to be urged and gave a speech on roughly the same lines as Lenin's. Then he led the Kronstadters towards the centre of the city, in the direction of the Tauride Palace. On the way this army was joined by the workers of the Trubochny and Baltic Factories. They were in a truculent mood. In the columns, headed by bands and surrounded by the curious, there was some extremely strong language directed at the Capitalist Ministers and the Compromisers of the Central Ex[ecutive] Com[mittee]. It was clear that Kronstadt had come out as one man to save the revolution, bringing ammunition and equipment; only the old and the young had been left at home.

But just where they were going or what for, they didn't really know. Lunacharsky had said he had "brought" the Kronstadters. But in my opinion they had got stuck somewhere on the Nevsky or near the Champ de Mars. I don't think Lunacharsky *brought* them to the Tauride Palace; as far as I remember they only appeared there around 5 o'clock in the afternoon.

The movement was also pouring out again apart from the Kronstadters. From the early morning the working-class districts were stirring. Around 11 o'clock a unit of the Volhynian Regiment "came out," followed by half the 180th, the whole 1st Machine-Gun Regiment and others. Around noon firing began at various points of the city—not skirmishes or fights, but firing: partly into the air, partly at people. There was shooting on the Suvorovsky Prospect, Basil Island, the Kamenno-ostrovsky, and especially on the Nevsky —near the Sadovoy and the Liteiny. As a rule it began with a chance shot; panic would follow; rifles began to go off at random. There were dead and wounded everywhere. . . .

There was absolutely no sign of any plan in the movement of the "insurrectionaries." But there could be no question of systematically localizing or liquidating the movement. The Soviet and Government authorities despatched loyal detachments of military cadets, Semyonovskys [Guards], and Cossacks. They paraded and encountered the enemy. But no one dreamed of a serious battle. At the first shot both sides panicked and scattered helter-skelter. Passers-by of course got the great bulk of the bullets. When two columns met each other neither participants nor spectators *could distinguish where either side was.* Perhaps only the Kronstadters had a distinctive look. As for the rest it was all muddle, spontaneous and irresistible. But the question is, were the first shots that started the panic and fighting accidental or not?

Small, isolated pogroms began. Because of shots from houses, or with them as a pretext, mass-searches were conducted by soldiers and sailors. The searches were a pretext for looting. Many shops suffered, mainly wine and food shops and tobacconists. Various groups began to arrest people on the streets at random.

Around 4 o'clock, according to rumour, the number of people wounded or killed already amounted to hundreds. Dead horses lay here and there. . . .

Around 7 o'clock, . . . suddenly like an arrow the news sped through the meeting: the men from the Putilov [machinery] Factory had come, 30,000 of them, bearing themselves extremely aggressively; some of them had burst into the Palace looking for Tsereteli [a leading Menshevik], who at that moment was not in the hall. They were said to have hunted all over the Palace for him without finding him. The hall was full of excitement, hubbub and frenzied yelling. Just then a crowd of about forty workers, many of them armed, burst in tempestuously. The deputies leaped from their seats. Some failed to show adequate courage and self-control.

One of the workers, a classical *sans-culotte,* in a cap and a short blue blouse without a belt, with a rifle in his hand, leaped up on to the speakers' platform. He was quivering with excitement and rage, stridently shouting out incoherent words and shaking his rifle:

"Comrades! How long must we workers put up with treachery? You're all here debating and making deals with the bourgeoisie and the landlords. . . . You're busy betraying the working class. Well, just understand that the working class won't put up with it! There are 30,000 of us all told here from Putilov. We're going to have our way. All power to the Soviets! We have a firm grip on our rifles! Your Kerenskys and Tseretelis are not going to fool us!"

Chkheidze [Chairman of the Soviet], in front of whose nose the rifle was dancing about, showed complete self-control. In answer to the hysterics of the *sans-culotte,* pouring out his hungry proletarian soul, the chairman tranquilly leaned down from his height and pushed into the worker's quivering hand a manifesto, printed the evening before:

"Here, please take this, Comrade, read it. It says here what you and your Putilov comrades should do. Please read it and don't interrupt our business. Everything necessary is said there."

The manifesto said that all those who had gone out into the street should go back home, otherwise they would be traitors to the revolution. The ruling Soviet clique and Chkheidze could think of nothing else to propose to the rank-and-file at a moment of extreme tension.

The baffled *sans-culotte*, not knowing what else to do, took the appeal and then without much difficulty was got off the platform. His comrades too were quickly "persuaded" to leave the hall. Order was restored and the incident liquidated. . . . But to this day I can still see that *sans-culotte* on the platform of the White Hall, shaking his rifle in self-oblivion in the faces of the hostile "leaders of the democracy," trying in torment to express the will, the longings, and the fury of the authentic proletarian lower depths, who scented treachery but were powerless to fight against it. This was one of the finest scenes of the revolution. And with Chkheidze's gesture one of the most dramatic.

b) The Provisional Government seized on the crisis of the July Days and the simultaneous appearance of charges that Lenin was in the pay of Germany, with the aim of breaking up the Bolshevik Party and apprehending its leaders. The party was virtually driven underground, and Lenin went into hiding to escape arrest.

The official charges were summarized in a press release on July 22, "Report of the Public Prosecutor on the Investigation of the Charges Against the Bolsheviks," from *The Russian Provisional Government, 1917: Documents,* Robert Paul Browder and Alexander F. Kerensky, eds. (Stanford, California: Stanford University Press, 1961), pp. 1373–76. © 1961 by the Board of Trustees of the Leland Stanford Junior University. This and the following selections from this volume are reprinted with the permission of the publisher.

Appeals to Armed Action

Definite data exist to the effect that the armed action on the part of military units on July 3–5 was far from a unanimous expression of their sentiment. Rather, it was artificially aroused by the incitement of individual leaders who, by means of demagogic and at times also provocative methods, set up intensive propaganda on the need to overthrow the government. These individuals advocated the disobedience of military units to commanding officers and refusal to go to the front to fight the enemy.

Investigation revealed that armed action was preceded by systematic meetings in military units where speeches were made urging the troops to revolt.

Thus, on July 2, the 1st Machine-Gun Regiment held a meeting and concert at the Narodnyi Dom where Lunacharsky, Trotsky, and others spoke. They all appealed for the overthrow of the Provisional Government, disobedience of military authorities, and refusal [to participate] in the offensive at the front. They pointed out that the offensive just concluded was the result of the deceiving actions of War Minister Kerensky and the officers and was the result of the arrival of the American capitalists [Root Mission?].

Trotsky's appeal, which tried to convince them of the necessity of armed action against the Government, aroused particular excitement. His speech was interrupted by cries: "Death to Kerensky," "Down with war," "Down with the capitalist ministers," "We don't need the offensive," "All power to the Soviet of Workers' and Soldiers' Deputies."

During the months of April, May, and June, Kolontai and Ensign Semashko attended the meetings of the Machine-Gun Regiment and spoke there. They urged the soldiers not to send companies to the front, not to obey the decisions of the regiment committees to send soldiers to the front, to overthrow the Provisional Government and thus achieve the transfer of all power to the Soviet of W. and S.D.

The Participation of the Central Committee of the Social Democratic Party in the Organization of the Revolt

It is established further that the revolt took place and continued according to the instructions of the Central Committee of the Social Democratic Party.

All leading instructions emanated from the house of Kshesinskaya, called by witnesses the "headquarters of Lenin." The Central Committee of the Social Democratic Party was also lodged there.

Forms of a military organization attached to the Central Committee of the Social Democratic Party were discovered in the house of Kshesinskaya. These were the very forms used for written instructions on armed action distributed in the army units.

It was on such a form that the Petrograd Military Automobile Shop received, during the night of July 4–5, a proposal to prepare armored cars for combat-readiness and to put them at the disposal of the Military Organization. The order to send a cruiser from Kronstadt was written on the same form.

Moreover, the following were also found there: (1) Notes on the distribution of military units and "armed workers" according to regions; on the distribution among various persons of responsibilities on "armed workers" according to regions; on the distribution among various persons of responsibilities on taking charge of armed forces, on reconnaissance, and outside watch; on contacts with units; on the Peter and Paul Fortress, on the military units comprising the Vyborg and Petrograd sections and Mars Field, and on establishing contacts with various regiments. (2) A resolution worked out at the session of the all-city conference of the Social Democratic Party and delegates from factories and military units on July 3, at 11:00 in the evening. The resolution recommended: "The immediate demonstration of workers and soldiers on the street in order to show their will." This resolution was signed by the Central Committee of the Social Democratic Party and the Military Organization of the S.D. Party. (3) A telegram from Stockholm, dated April 20, addressed to Ulianov (Lenin) and signed by Ganetsky (Fürstenberg): "Steinberg will try to get a subsidy for our organization. I must request his action be controlled, because social tact is completely lacking." (4) Literature of the "Union of the Russian People" [an extreme right-wing organization] and a large number of postal cards, published by *"Pauk"* [Spider] and illustrating [an alleged Jewish] ritual murder in Hungary in 1882.

The relation between the armed insurrection and the activity of the Central Committee of the S.D. Party, which maintained a military organization, is established, in addition to documentary data, by the fact that the armed units which participated in the insurrection, both from the Petrograd garrison and from Kronstadt, proceeded to the house of Kshesinskaya, where they received instructions from Ulianov (Lenin) and other persons. Suggestions to the military units about battle-readiness of armored cars and machine guns also emanated from there, and, finally, it was there that the armored trucks and automobiles gathered.

AID TO THE ENEMY AND ESPIONAGE

The intensive propaganda campaign for an insurrection, which was waged among the troops and the civilian population over several months and which resulted in the insurrection of July 3–5, was staged for the purpose of aiding the enemy in its hostile actions against Russia.

In this connection data have been obtained by the investigation indicating that a large espionage organization working for Germany exists in Russia. But in the interests of the investigation only the following data are released thus far:

A number of witnesses questioned in the case attested that while residing in the German part of Switzerland, Lenin was in contact with Parvus (he also being Helfand), who had the definite reputation of being a German agent; that Lenin frequented the camps for the Ukrainian prisoners, where he carried on propaganda for the separation of the Ukraine from Russia.

EVIDENCE POINTING TO LENIN AS A GERMAN AGENT

The data of the preliminary investigation point directly to Lenin as a German agent and indicate that, after entering into an agreement with Germany on action designed to aid Germany in her war with Russia, he arrived in Petrograd. Here, with financial assistance from Germany, he began to act to achieve this aim.

RELATIONS WITH GERMANY

Relations with Germany were carried on through Stockholm. In April of this year an attempt was made from Stockholm to publish outside of Petrograd a newspaper for the purpose of waging a campaign against England and France.

Large sums of money appeared among the German agents in Copenhagen and Stockholm in the early days of the revolution, and an extensive recruiting of agents for Russia was launched among our deserters and emigrants. Sums of money (800 thousand rubles, 250 thousand rubles, and other sums) were remitted to Russia from Stockholm through one bank which received orders from Germany.

It was also revealed that Lenin and Zinoviev, while living in Austria near Krakow, were arrested in October 1914 by the Austrian authorities as Russian subjects, but were soon released with the right of free departure for Switzerland, where they started publication of the journal *Sotsial-Demokrat,* which advocated the idea of the necessity of Russia's defeat in the present war.

An important role in freeing Zinoviev and Lenin was played by Ganetsky, who, according to his own words, told one of the witnesses to "break off" the examination of Lenin and Zinoviev by the Austrian authorities. It was subsequently revealed that Lenin and Zinoviev were released from Austrian arrest by personal order of Count Stürgkh, the Austrian Prime Minister.

The investigation established that Yakov (diminutive "Kuba") Ganetsky-Fürstenberg, while residing in Copenhagen during the war, was closely connected in financial matters with Parvus, agent of the German government.

Moreover, the activity of Parvus as a German and Austrian agent was directed toward the defeat of Russia and its separation from the Ukraine.

The investigation established that Kozlovsky traveled from Copenhagen, where he represented himself as legal adviser to the prominent capitalist Helfand. Helfand (Parvus) proposed the financing of a steamship company in Russia. During the negotiations in this connection it was revealed that Parvus had at his disposal a large amount of capital, but was completely ignorant of the business which he proposed to finance.

On making inquiries the representatives of the steamship company learned that Helfand had over a million rubles in a bank in Copenhagen.

When it became clear to the representatives of the steamship company that the business activity of Helfand (Parvus) was merely a cover-up for his work for Germany, they ended all negotiations with him.

Simultaneously with this it was revealed that Helfand-Parvus, together with Fürstenberg and Kozlovsky, made trips from Copenhagen to Berlin and back.

HELFAND-PARVUS, LENIN, AND OTHERS

From the numerous telegrams in the hands of the legal authorities it is established that a constant and extensive correspondence was carried on between Sumenson, Ulianov (Lenin),

Kollontai, and Kozlovsky, residing in Petrograd, on the one hand, and Fürstenberg (Ganetsky) and Helfand (Parvus), on the other. Although this correspondence refers to commercial deals, shipment of all sorts of goods, and money transactions, it offers sufficient reasons to conclude that this correspondence was a cover-up for relations of an espionage character.

According to data in this matter, it is clear that some Russian banks received large sums, paid to various people, from Scandinavian banks. And it is interesting that within half a year Sumenson withdrew from her personal account 750,000 rubles deposited to her credit by various persons and that the current balance on her account is 180,000 rubles.

THE FORTHCOMING INVESTIGATION

In investigating the present case the inquest authorities are guided by the materials secured only through inquest, and this material gives entirely sufficient reason to brand the action as criminal as well as to uncover many of the persons who participated in it. The forthcoming numerous cross-examinations of witnesses, examination of material evidence found, detailed investigation of money transactions—all this complex work of the future should yield abundant material uncovering the criminal espionage organization and its participants.

In reviewing all of the indicated questions, the inquest authorities were concerned, not with the political platforms of the persons involved, but only in uncovering criminal activity and finding sufficient grounds for prosecuting the accused.

CONCLUSION

On the basis of the data outlined, as well as of data that cannot as yet be made public, Vladimir Ulianov (Lenin), Ovsei-Gersh Arenov Apfelbaum (Zinoviev), Alexandra Mikhailovna Kollontai, Mecheslav Ulievich Kozlovsky, Evgenia Mavrikievna Sumenson, Helfand (Parvus), Yakov Fürstenberg (Kuba Ganetsky), Midshipman Ilin (Raskolnikov), and Ensigns Semashko, Sakharov, and Roshal are accused of having entered—in 1917, while Russian citizens, by a preliminary agreement between themselves and other persons, and for the purpose of aiding the enemy countries at war with Russia—with said countries into an agreement to assist in the disorganization of the Russian army and the rear in order to weaken the fighting strength of the army. For this purpose and with the money received from said states, they organized propaganda among the civilian population and in the army, appealing to them to refuse immediately to continue military actions against the enemy; also, toward the same end, to organize in Petrograd, from July 3 to 5, 1917, an armed insurrection against the existing order in the state supreme authority. This was accompanied by murders and violence and attempts to arrest some members of the Government. As a consequence of this, some military units refused to carry out orders of their commanding personnel and arbitrarily abandoned their positions, thus aiding in the success of the enemy's armies.

The Kornilov Movement

One of Kerensky's first moves after being installed as Prime Minister of the Provisional Government on July 8 was to appoint General Lavr Kornilov, hero of the June offensive, as Commander-in-Chief of the army. Bent on repairing the damage done to military discipline by the influence of the soviets, Kornilov attracted the support of counter-revolutionaries and the suspicion of the Kerensky government. Tempted by the unauthorized encouragement of a cabinet minister, V. N. Lvov, Kornilov ordered his troops to march on Petrograd to install a government of national salvation. The move nevertheless collapsed as Kornilov's forces deserted, leaving the Right discredited, the government enfeebled, and the door open to the Left.

The following documents are from Browder and Kerensky, *The Russian Provisional Government*, pp. 1563–65, 1572–73.

a) Memoirs of V. N. Lvov

. . . It was 10:00 o'clock in the evening [of August 24] when I entered Kornilov's office. I greeted him and said:
"I come from Kerensky."
Kornilov's eyes sparkled with an evil glint.

"I have a proposal to make to you," I continued. "It is wrongly believed that Kerensky is anxious to stay in power. He is ready to resign if he is in your way. But the power must be legally transferred from hand to hand. The power cannot be abandoned, but neither can it be seized. Kerensky has agreed to reorganize the Government so as to draw all elements of society into it. This is my proposal— an agreement with Kerensky."

Kornilov calmed down and replied:

"I have nothing against Kerensky. When he wanted to resign at the Moscow State Conference, I advised him against it. Then he asked me whether I would support him, and I promised him my support. But, then, Kerensky does not fight against the Bolsheviks. Days go by and he does nothing in this respect. This is wrong. If a Bolshevik uprising occurs in Petrograd, there will be an incredible mess. I was commander of the Petrograd forces and I know the mood of those men. Some of the regiments will support the Bolsheviks, others will be against it. In this mess the Provisional Government will perish. This must not happen. Some action must be taken to prevent this. I know Kerensky, and I know that one can reach an understanding with him. But Kerensky is hated and I cannot vouch for his life. Today Savinkov [deputy War Minister under Kerensky] came here to complain to me about the Soviet. What can I do when I cannot get the Government to place under my command all the troops at the front and in the rear? Regimental committees interfere with military orders. However, I cannot complain about them as far as the economic [side of the question] is concerned: in this respect they are useful. But come at 10:00 o'clock tomorrow morning for the final answer."

I left, fully satisfied that Kornilov was in favor of an agreement. . . .

At 10:00 A.M. on the following day (August 25) I was going up the stairs of the Governor's house where Kornilov was located, when an elderly enlistee met me on the top flight. He was a tall, stout man; his hair was dark with streaks of gray. He introduced himself: "Zavoiko." Zavoiko apologized on behalf of the Supreme Commander for asking me to wait. . . .

I entered Kornilov's office and sat down by his side at the desk. Kornilov started speaking to me in a firm and assured manner. The hesitating tone of yesterday was no longer evident.

"Tell Kerensky," Kornilov said to me, "that Riga fell because the draft bills I submitted to the Provisional Government have still not been approved. The fall of Riga arouses the indignation of the whole army. There can be no further delay. Regimental committees must have no right to interfere with military orders; Petrograd must be included in the sphere of military operations and placed under martial law; all units of the front and the rear must be subordinated to the Supreme Commander. From counterintelligence reports submitted to me, the Bolsheviks are planning to stage an uprising in Petrograd between August 28 and September 2. The aim of this uprising is to overthrow the Provisional Government, proclaim the power of the Soviet, conclude peace with Germany, and give up the Baltic Fleet to Germany. . . . In view of such a formidable threat to Russia, I can see no other way out than to transfer the power of the Provisional Government to . . . the Supreme Commander."

I interrupted Kornilov.

"The transfer of military power alone, or civil as well?" I asked.

"Both military and civil," Kornilov explained.

"Allow me to write all this down so as to remember it."

"Please," said Kornilov, and offered me a pencil and paper.

"Perhaps it would be better simply to combine the office of Supreme Commander with the office of President of the Council of Ministers," I interposed.

Kornilov was embarrassed.

"Possibly your scheme is also acceptable," said Kornilov.

"Of course, all this is before the Constituent Assembly," Kornilov remarked.

"Furthermore," he continued, "warn Kerensky and Savinkov that I cannot vouch for their lives . . . , and, therefore, let them come to Stavka [Headquarters] where I will personally be responsible for their safety."

I was moved by these words . . . and said to Kornilov:

"You are an honorable man."

Kornilov continued:

"It is not my concern who will be the Supreme Commander as long as the Provisional Government transfers the power to him."

I said to Kornilov:

"If it's a question of a military dictatorship, then who is to be the dictator, if not you?"

Kornilov nodded and continued:

"At any rate, if the Romanovs rise to the throne, it will only be over my dead body. As soon as the power is transferred, I will form my cabinet.

"I no longer trust Kerensky, he is not doing anything."

"And do you trust Savinkov?" I asked.

"No. I do not trust Savinkov either. I don't know whom he wants to stab in the back. It could be Kerensky, it could be me," Kornilov replied.

"If you have such an opinion of Savinkov, why didn't you arrest him yesterday while he was here?"

Kornilov was silent.

"However," Kornilov continued, "I could offer Savinkov the portfolio of Minister of War, and Kerensky—the portfolio of Minister of Justice."

At this point, to my complete surprise, Zavoiko . . . entered the office unannounced, interrupted the Supreme Commander, and said in a tone that teachers use toward pupils:

"No, no, not Minister of Justice, but Vice-President of the Council of Ministers."

I looked in amazement first at Kornilov, then at the orderly. Kornilov appeared disconcerted.

"Then is it your wish that I relay all this to Kerensky?" I asked Kornilov.

Zavoiko answered:

"Of course, of course, legal succession of power is important."

"In this case," I turned to Kornilov, "would you reserve a seat for me on the train since no tickets are being sold?"

Zavoiko said that he would personally accompany me to the station and arrange everything.

I bade farewell to Kornilov and left the office.

Zavoiko invited me for lunch at his place; he was located in the same building. I entered his place and found Dobrynsky and another gentleman whom I had not met. . . . Zavoiko introduced us:

"Professor Yakovlev."

Then Zavoiko sat at the desk, took out a piece of paper on which something was written, and began reading aloud. It was Kornilov's manifesto to the army in which Kornilov, calling himself a son of a Cossack, was taking Supreme Power in the name of saving the native land. Then . . . Zavoiko pulled out another paper from the desk and started reading. That was Kornilov's proclamation to the soldiers. It promised 8 dessiatines of land [about 20 acres] to every soldier when he returned home. This turned out to be the agrarian program drawn up by Professor Yakovlev who was sitting before me.

"Where are you going to find so many dessiatines for every soldier?" I asked.

Yakovlev explained that he had everything calculated precisely.

After reading the manifesto and the proclamation, Zavoiko slipped me a copy of each. I put them automatically into my pocket without knowing why he gave them to me. Then, taking a piece of paper with a casual air, Zavoiko said:

"And so, the Vice-President of the Council of Ministers will be Kerensky."

b) Radio-Telegram from Kerensky to All the Country

I hereby announce:

On August 26 General Kornilov sent to me member of the State Duma Vladimir Lvov with a demand for the surrender by the Provisional Government of all civil and military power, so that he may form, at his personal discretion, a *new government* to administer the country. The authenticity of Deputy Lvov's authorization to make such a proposal to me was subsequently confirmed by General Kornilov in his conversation with me by direct wire. Perceiving in the presentation of such demands, addressed to the Provisional Government in my person, a desire of certain circles of Russian society to take advantage of the grave condition of the State for the purpose of establishing in the country a regime opposed to the conquests of the revolution, the Provisional Government has found it indispensable:

To authorize me, for the salvation of our motherland, of liberty, and of our republican order, to take prompt and resolute measures for the purpose of uprooting any attempt to encroach upon the Supreme Power in the State and upon the rights which the citizens have achieved by the revolution.

I am taking all necessary measures to protect the liberty and order of the country, and the population will be informed in due time with regard to such measures.

At the same time I order herewith:

1. General Kornilov to surrender the post of Supreme Commander to General Klembovsky, the Commander-in-Chief of the Northern

Front, which bars the way to Petrograd; and General Klembovsky to assume temporarily the post of Supreme Commander, while remaining at Pskov.

2. The city and uezd [district] of Petrograd under martial law, extending to it the regulations for regions declared under martial law. . . .

I call upon all the citizens to preserve complete tranquillity and to maintain order, which is so indispensable for the salvation of the country. I call upon all the ranks of the army and navy to carry on with calmness and self-sacrifice their duty of defending the country against the external enemy.

> A. F. KERENSKY,
> Minister-President,
> Minister of War and Navy
> August 27, 1917

c) Kornilov's Response to Kerensky's Radio-Telegram

The Minister-President's telegram No. 4163 in its entire first part is a lie throughout: it was not I who sent the Member of the State Duma, Vladimir Lvov, to the Provisional Government, but he came to me as the envoy of the Minister-President. Aleksei Aladin, Member of the State Duma, is a witness to this. A *great provocation* has thus taken place which jeopardizes the fate of the motherland.

People of Russia! Our great motherland is dying. The hour of her death is near. Forced to speak openly, I, General Kornilov, declare that under the pressure of the Bolshevik majority of the Soviets, the Provisional Government acts in complete harmony with the plans of the German general staff, and simultaneously with the forthcoming landing of the enemy forces on the Riga shores, it is killing the army and undermines the very foundation of the country.

The heavy sense of the inevitable ruin of the country commands me in these ominous moments to call upon all Russian people to come to the aid of the dying motherland. All in whose breasts a

Russian heart is beating, who believe in God, in Church, pray to the Lord for the greatest miracle, the saving of our native land!

I, General Kornilov, son of a Cossack peasant, declare to all and sundry that I want nothing for myself, except the preservation of a Great Russia, and I vow to bring the people by means of victory over the enemy to the Constituent Assembly, where they will themselves decide their fate and choose their new form of government. But it is quite impossible for me to betray Russia into the hands of her ancient enemy, the German race, and to turn the Russian people into German slaves. I prefer to die on the battlefield of honor rather than see the disgrace and infamy of the Russian land.

Russian people, the life of your motherland is in your hands!

GENERAL KORNILOV.

August 27, 1917

Part Three
🐚 THE SOCIAL REVOLUTION

Caught in the turmoil of contending parties and factions, the Russian Provisional Government quickly lost touch with the mood of most segments of the Russian population in their aspirations for revolutionary justice. The economic dislocations bequeathed by Tsarism steadily worsened, and with inflation and food shortages the urban working class was rapidly radicalized. The army succumbed to a profound spirit of democratization that made military discipline impossible, and that rendered it nearly impotent as a fighting force even before the peasant soldiers began deserting to go home and join in the seizure of the land. The Russian villages were in the throes of revolution by fall, as the peasants, impatient of the government's paralytic legalism, began solving the land problem themselves by direct action against the landlords. Finally, the non-Russian minorities of the borderlands, especially the Finns and the Ukrainians, took advantage of the weakness of the Provisional Government to try to realize their dreams of self-determination. Everywhere the scene of social revolution showed growing violence and deepening anarchy, a condition which only the most ruthless and efficient authority could rectify.

Economic Breakdown

The combined dislocations of war and revolution intensified the critical economic situation that had underlain the February Revolution. Inflation accelerated, strikes disrupted industry, transportation broke down, and the normal relations of exchange between city and countryside were ruptured. In turn, economic difficulties intensified the revolutionary mood of the country, particularly as the food supply failed.

The Provisional Government's Minister of Food Supply, A. V. Peshekhonov, made a gloomy report on the situation to the First Congress of Soviets in May, 1917. This document is contained in Browder and Kerensky, *The Russian Provisional Government,* pp. 633–36.

When the revolution broke out, it may be said that we were already in the midst of a food crisis. There were hardly any grain reserves left in the large towns and in the army. One had to live from day to day in the first months of the revolution. But still it must be said that the country exhibited confidence in the new order. In general the supply of grain in the month of March was much better than in February, the last month under the old regime. There were hopes that supplies would increase even more. But then, in April, a big delay in the supply of grain occurred. A whole set of circumstances was involved here: the spring season for bad roads, and the Easter celebration, and the overflow of rivers. In addition, with the onset of spring, certain railroad bridges were damaged, and the spring sowing, with which our comrade peasants should occupy themselves [was spoiled]. All this led to the fact that in April the rate of grain supply sharply declined and, finally, fell to 5,000,000 poods[1] per week, while the needs of the army, the towns, and the consumer population required 17,000,000 poods per week.

The situation became more and more critical and menacing. Moscow, in particular, was left almost without grain. Petrograd also existed on a day-to-day basis. It must be said that by May the situation improved considerably. The amount of grain conveyed to the stations and delivered by the peasants had increased. We are now in a position to supply the army with sufficient quantities of grain. Any delays at the present time are due to the condition of the railroads. This, by the way, accounts for the fact that only very recently the Northern Front experienced the most serious difficulties with food supply. There was grain to be shipped from Rybinsk and Nizhni, but the railroads were unable to transport it. Only very recently did they succeed in doing so. The delivery of grain to the stations continues, the stations are provided for, and although the norm has not yet been reached, we are able, according to rough estimates, to supply the army and the large towns, and later, in

[1] [One pood = 36 lbs.—ED.]

June or July, we will be able to provide for other needy areas. There are very serious apprehensions now concerning August, because harvest time will begin at the end of June and the conveyance of grain to the stations will diminish once again. But, at any rate, one cannot consider the situation to be extremely desperate or extremely dangerous.

Concerning the outlook for the future, the situation is as follows: there was, indeed, a decrease of sowing in certain areas, but, in general, one may consider that there was no decrease in the crop area and that, in fact, the crop area increased in certain areas. . . .

From the very beginning of the war we had an absolute shortage of certain food products. From the very beginning we were short of groats. This shortage still exists and it will probably be impossible to meet this demand completely in the future. Similarly, there is a shortage of many meat and fat products. In this respect the population must continue to endure scarcity and must sharply reduce its needs.

The staple food—grain—still does not cause particular apprehension, judging by the quantity of grain available in the country. But the problem lies in obtaining and conveying this grain. It must be said at this point that we have already encountered great difficulties in solving this problem in the past and that we may again encounter great difficulties in the future.

As you know, an attempt at taking grain by the old system, with the help of the commercial machinery, has been completely discredited during the war. No, it is impossible to live by the old ways when the dealers obtained the grain for us, collected it, and delivered it to us. Even the former government was forced to come to this conclusion. It was forced to supply more and more grain to the army, and then to the population, bypassing the dealers. During the war we were forced to come to the conclusion that even the slightest participation of dealers led to a sharp and rapid increase in prices. The people began to be very reluctant to give up the grain, saying: Why should we give our grain today when the price on it will be still higher tomorrow? Speculation began to run high; it was followed by bribery, graft in the railroads, and [the appearance of] "pushers." We have been convinced of this sufficiently not to return to the system and, furthermore, to repudiate it firmly. The Provisional Government decided to reject it and to abolish entirely the role of private commerce in supplying the country with grain.

Now another problem is how to take the grain from the people so that the same dealers will be prevented from taking it, while the grain, all the grain, has been declared the property of the State. But it will only become the property of the State when it can be registered, and in order to register this state grain and turn it over to the army or to the needy areas, food committees have been instituted. But until these food committees are established throughout the guberniyas [provinces], uezds [counties], and volosts [townships], there is no possibility of registering it. And, it must be said, one of the principal difficulties of the present time is that these committees are not being established as quickly as was expected, and the general impression is as follows: in areas where there is shortage of grain, where grain must be distributed, there the committees have sprung up very quickly, but in areas from which grain must be obtained, where it must be given up, the committees are very slow in becoming established. . . .

. . . And now, comrades, we are facing the most difficult problem of all. Formerly grain was taken in exchange for money, but now the people have almost no desire to give up the grain for money, because money is cheap, and the peasantry is holding on to the one thing that, so to speak, it has in its hands, and the people simply have no desire to receive money with which one cannot buy anything while the prices on all manufactured goods and on all products are rising so fast.

Therefore, in order to assure grain supplies from the village for the army and the towns, there remains one task for the Government and for the Ministry of Food: that of assuring the peasantry that it shall receive from the towns the products it needs. . . .

The basic difficulty is this: the town lacks the products that could be given to the village in exchange for grain. . . . Even if we hold the prices down in one way or another, even if we do not allow them to spiral, the basic problem remains that there is a shortage of very many products in the country. . . .

And now, comrades, the problem is reduced to two points: . . . the first task is to establish an even distribution of all the products in short supply.

The other task, comrades, is even more serious and difficult: to increase our production, to try, nevertheless, to increase these products as much as possible and to direct all our efforts in this direction. And so, it must be said that in this respect the problem is an especially difficult one. The economic machinery upon which our production depends has been shaken: in one place there is a shortage of coal—this causes production to stop; in another place there may be sufficient coal, but there is a shortage of metals; in a third place there is still another reason, and, consequently, it often happens that our production is lower than the efforts we put into it; but there is still one other very serious reason, and I have decided to speak frankly about it here. Comrades, the manpower we have at our disposal is not utilized sufficiently well. It has already been noted before that the old government conscripted a great many more people into the army than was necessary, and there is no doubt that there are too many men in the army now, especially in the rear, who essentially remain with nothing to do. To utilize this manpower is one of the tasks that confront us.

Another problem, which is again difficult to approach, is the decline in the productivity of our workers. Once again we must admit that productivity has fallen during the revolutionary period; we found ourselves in a situation where our productivity was declining just at a time when there was a great scarcity of products. Comrades, the matter stands as follows: in the course of many, many years our working class was under pressure and this pressure was particularly pronounced during the war period. The working class had to work beyond measure while the wages were far from commensurate with the labor or [proportionate] to the national income. . . . This was prior to the revolution. As you know, the correlation of forces has changed since the revolution: the workers received an opportunity to demand better conditions for themselves, with respect both to working hours and to wages; but the workers' movement turned out to be much stronger and much more widespread than our material opportunities could afford. A considerable part of the working class reasoned that since it was possible to make demands, and since these demands could be fulfilled, then it followed that they should be made and, moreover, they should be vast and significant in scope.

. . . Comrades, the principal difficulty we confront in resolving this problem is our difficulty with you and with the masses which stand behind you. Comrades, the resistance of the capitalists has apparently been broken. Evidently, it is possible to strike at them and to go very far in this direction, almost to the expropriation of all profits; at least, some delegates came to us and said: "We are ready to give up all our profits if only we can preserve our industry." Even more than that, many came and said: "Take our enterprises, we are giving them away—please, manage them yourselves." In addition, . . . the Government is very willing to go firmly in this direction.

But, comrades, this alone is not enough. It is also necessary that the popular masses understand, realize, and feel that they too must be called upon to make sacrifices. They must realize that under the present conditions it is impossible to satisfy demands completely, that under these conditions one must try to prevent anyone from taking more than his allotted share, so that the distribution among the masses will be as even as possible. But one cannot go and try to obtain better terms now; one must only try to achieve an equitable distribution, on the one hand, and, on the other hand, to call on the popular masses to exert every effort to increase production in the interest of improving the position of the workers. This, comrades, is what we should strive for, this is the course we must follow. Until such time as we reach this awareness, all our hopes for adjusting the economy will be unattainable.

The Workers' Revolution

Radical tradition, economic conditions, and frustration at the stance of the Provisional Government and the industrialists combined during 1917 to generate accelerating revolutionary sentiment among the industrial workers, above all in Petrograd. The drive for class power crystallized in the movement to create "Factory and Mill Committees."

a)Appeal to Factory and Mill Workers' Committees, Councils of Elders, Railroad and Transport Workers*

* Issued by the Organizational Bureau of the First Conference of Factory and Mill Committees, May, 1917; published in V. L. Meller and A. M. Pankratova, eds., *Rabochee Dvizhenie v 1917 g.* [The Workers' Movement in 1917] (Moscow and Leningrad: State Press, 1926), pp. 75–77. (Editor's translation.)

Comrades! With each passing day all Russia is moving closer and closer to economic collapse. The factories and mills face the possibility of shutting down, since there is neither solid nor liquid fuel, there are no raw materials, movement on the railroads is in disorder, there are not enough locomotives and cars. The tsarist government and the capitalists, who dragged Russia into this most terrible war, cared only about their profits and not about organizing the country's work in the factories, mills, railroads, steamships and other enterprises and trades.

As a result of this criminal behavior Russia is on the eve of a grave economic crisis. The work of the factories and mills may stop and then millions of workers and peasants, above all, will suffer— they will be thrown out onto the streets, unemployed. And the Russian Revolution, which is still going on, is in danger.

The Revolution still has to end the war and transfer all the land to the whole people. The Revolution must also decide the workers question and many other different ones. All this has not yet been done, but remains to be done by the workers, soldiers, and peasants in the course of the Russian Revolution. But its success is completely dependent on whether it will succeed in ruling out economic collapse, whether it will succeed in arranging all industrial life so that everything is in proper order, the factories and mills are working, the railroads are operating properly, cars and locomotives are available, and the workers and employees are not thrown out onto the street into the realm of Tsar Hunger. And if at the present time when the whole of life is tailored for wartime the workers are threatened by the danger of turning up in the position of the unemployed, this question will become especially acute the moment peace is concluded.

Before Russian industry stands the question of the reconversion of production from war to peace, i.e., the question of the demobilization of industry. Cannons, shrapnel, explosives, and all the other things necessary for war are unnecessary in peacetime. And all the workers who are making these things will also be thrown out onto the street. For this not to happen, it is essential for the working class to assume the most direct participation in the reconversion of production, i.e., in the demobilization of industry.

All this can be accomplished only with the participation of the organized toilers, who everywhere in the provinces must convoke committees and take the most active, effective participation in the life of the given enterprise. Such committees already exist in many factories and mills in Petrograd and other cities. But if they work separated from each other, without a common direction, disunited, they will not constitute such a force as could intervene in the economic life of revolutionary Russia and thereby lead it out of the blind alley which it is getting more and more deeply into every day.

Powerful and strong organizations of the toilers themselves must undertake this work. They who stand at the work bench have to save revolutionary Russia. And for this it is necessary above all for all workers' factory and mill committees, councils of elders, railroad workers' and transportation committees to merge together and form a powerful economic organization, and together with the workers' trade unions, cooperative organizations and labor exchanges, to undertake promptly the control and regulation of industry and rule out economic collapse. Only by intervening in the economic life of Russia can we save the Revolution from ruin. And as long as the Revolution is in danger, we toilers cannot be at ease.

Comrades, prepare for the All-Russian Congress of Workers' Committees! If anywhere among the factories and mills and other industrial enterprises such committees have not yet been formed, hasten to organize them. Do not delay even for a minute. For any delay here threatens our revolution and our freedom. Remember that the cause of the working class is in its own hands, and in making the future development of our revolution secure, we come nearer to the end of fratricidal butchery, and to international socialism, i.e., our final goal.

In the next few days a conference (congress) of mill committees of the city of Petrograd will be held, after which will follow the All-Russian Congress. The date of the conference will be announced in all the socialist newspapers.

Come, comrades, in full awareness of the great work lying before us, to the task of uniting all workers' and employees' committees, first in Petrograd and then all over Russia.

Prepare, comrades, for the coming conference, and consider the following agenda:

1. The state of industry in Petrograd.
2. Control and regulation of production and the course of work in the enterprises.
3. Tasks of the factory and mill committees.
4. Unemployment and the demobilization of industry.

5. The role of mill committees in the trade union movement.

6. Attitude toward the labor exchanges and cooperatives.

7. Formation of a unifying economic center under the central trade unions.

b) Speech of Minister of Trade and Industry A. I. Konovalov to the Congress of War Industry Committees, Moscow, May 18, 1917*

Without false shame, frankly and honestly we must recognize that a difficult task lies ahead of us, that the task which awaits an urgent solution from us is absolutely exceptional in its magnitude and difficulty. . . . Inside the country, have we ever been as close to a catastrophe which is ready to shatter to its foundations and to annihilate our entire economic life, and which at the present time we are approaching? The slogans which are being thrust into the midst of the workers, exciting the dark instincts of the mob, are followed by destruction, anarchy, and the annihilation of public and national life. Under the influence of this agitation on the part of irresponsible individuals, the working masses put forward demands whose realization would mean the complete destruction of enterprises. The conscious kindling of passions is being carried on systematically and insistently; demands are incessantly followed by new ones, the form of their presentation taking an ever more insufferable and inadmissible character. The regular course of activity of industrial enterprises has become severely hindered, and it is necessary to exert to the extreme the energy of the nation in order to master the disintegration, to safeguard the country from economic ruin, and to maintain at the required level the cause of national defense. When overthrowing the old regime we firmly believed that under the conditions of freedom a mighty development of the productive forces lay before the country, but at the present moment it is not so much a question of thinking about developing productive forces as to exert every effort in order to save from complete destruction all the embryos of industrial life that existed in the difficult atmosphere of the old regime. And if in the near future a sobering up of the befogged minds does not take place,

* Browder and Kerensky, *The Russian Provisional Government,* pp. 668–69.

if the people do not understand that they are chopping off the branch on which they are sitting, if the leading elements of the Soviet of Workers' and Soldiers' Deputies do not manage to master the movement and to direct it into the channel of legitimate class struggle, then we shall witness the stopping of scores and hundreds of enterprises. We shall witness the complete paralysis of economic life and shall enter into a long period of irreparable economic catastrophe, when millions of people will find themselves without work, without bread, without a roof, and when the agony of production will embrace one branch of the national economy after another, bringing with it everywhere death, destruction, and misery, partly shattering credit and provoking financial crises and everybody's ruin. Only then will the popular masses understand into what an abyss they have allowed themselves to be drawn, but then it will be too late. The State cannot take upon itself the obligation to give to the working class an exclusively privileged position at the expense of the whole population. The Provisional Government seeks measures for the earliest possible de-electrification of the atmosphere which has now been created between the representatives of labor and of capital. At the same time, the Government is looking for general measures directed toward regulating national economic life as a whole. The Government expects assistance, requests energetic support from all those to whom the success of the revolutionary cause in Russia is dear. If the Government possesses the necessary plenitude of power, if the feeling of personal responsibility for the fate of Russia is recognized by everyone, then I have no doubt that Russia will emerge completely victorious from all the dangers that are threatening her at the present moment.

c) *Resolution of the Third Conference of Factory and Mill Committees of Petrograd (September, 1917, "On the Question of the Campaign against the Factory and Mill Committees"* *

Having considered the question of the campaign against the factory–plant committees on the part of the organized industrialists, and the policy of the Ministry of Labor in this area, the

* Meller and Pankratova, pp. 119–124. (Editor's translation.)

Third City Conference of Factory and Mill Committees of Petrograd declares:

The implementation of the order of the Chief Committee of United Industry on terminating as of September 15 payment for the work of workers occupied in the mill committees, and of the circulars of the Ministry of Labor of August 28 and 29, which upheld it and limited the freedom of meetings and suppressed committee meetings on company time—threaten to destroy these committees and strike a terrible blow at the work of all other workers' organizations.

Production is collapsing. The criminal rapacious policy of the capitalists, leading to the aggravation of this collapse with the aim of stifling the Revolution, sets before the working class, which is at the present time the most interested in guaranteeing the possibility of a normal course for the economic and industrial life of the country, the task of organizing production, shaken by the war and consciously disrupted by the capitalists, and the task of controlling production and distribution. The most direct and near-by organs of this control in each place are the factory and mill committees, which have been created in the course of the Revolution. Sabotage by the capitalists and the economic breakdown into which the economic and political domination of the bourgeoisie has pushed the country place before the working class the unavoidable task of taking into its hands by means of a series of measures the control and regulation, and ultimately the organization, of the economic system. It is forming and strengthening its own special organs for this work, the factory and mill committees, which will act in close agreement with all other workers' organizations.

At the present time, a time when the Counter-revolution is growing stronger, when the collapse is reaching the highest degree, when a series of mass lay-offs is being noted, when a series of mills has been marked for closing and evacuation [out of Petrograd], intensive, uninterrupted and diverse work of the mill committees and their central councils is essential.

Under such circumstances the campaign against these committees is a direct crime against the Revolution. And the solidarity of the Ministry of Labor with the Chief Committee of United Industry in this criminal campaign must appear to the working class as one more stern lesson of the ruinousness of the policy of compromise [with the bourgeoisie].

Even on the formal side, the circular of the Ministry of Labor of August 28, in the part that suppresses meetings of the committee, is a violation of that same law of April 23 of this year which this circular is elucidating. In §7 of said law it is stated that the conditions and arrangements for releasing from work the people elected by the workers are established by instructions that are worked out by the mill committee and specify the composition, objectives, and line of action of the committee.

Section 8 merely requires the mutual agreement of both sides on this question.

The action of the Ministry of Labor aimed at extirpating the mill committee is not confined to the circulars cited here. In the Ministry of Labor the draft of a new law on hiring has been worked out, and in this draft not a word is said about the mill committee—they are putting them outside the law—while points 16 and 19 set up and confirm the prerevolutionary "autocracy" of entrepreneurs in defining internal arrangements in mills and factories.

Proceeding from the foregoing and clearly recognizing that only the removal of the counter-revolutionary bourgeoisie from power and the termination of the opportunity for it to utilize the machinery of governmental power for its plundering class purposes offers a real guarantee of the unimpeded planned development of workers' organizations, the conference seeks:

1. The immediate cancellation of the circulars of the Ministry of Labor of August 28 and 29.

2. Confirmation by legislative arrangement of the rights of factory and mill committees, which they enjoy at the present time on the basis of the rights of revolutionary custom.

3. To instruct the central council to seek a review and working out of a new law on hiring.

4. To continue the work of the factory and mill committees at each place on the former basis, deepening and broadening them in the direction of establishing real workers' control over production and distribution.

5. Not to allow removal of comrades serving on the committee from the payroll, and to demand payment to them of their average earnings.

The Soldiers' Revolution

The mood of revolutionary democracy engendered by the February Revolution rapidly spread to the front-line army, with a plethora of committees and commissars. To those officials like V. B. Stankevich, political commissar of the Provisional Government for the Northern Front, nearest Petrograd, who were committed to the defense of the country, it was a superhuman task to suppress the infection of revolution.

Stankevich describes the difficulties in his *Vospominaniya 1914–1919 gg.* [Memoirs, 1914–1919] (Berlin: Ladyzhnikov, 1920), pp. 182–84, 186–90. (Editor's translation.)

The main difficulty was, of course, not with the commanding staff but with the mass of soldiers.

In order to judge the mood of the masses, it is necessary first of all to remember clearly all the extraordinary and unusual character of that phenomenon which our army represented, even when evaluated on the scale of world history.

From the darkness of the old discipline, mechanical behavior, and undeniable subservience, an army that quantitatively exceeded the hordes of Attila by fifteen times had suddenly entered into another world. It was blinded by the possibilities opening before it, deafened by the stream of slogans, programs, appeals, speeches, resounding everywhere, uncomprehended, strange, but provoking great and unexpected thoughts.

For the soldier, ordinarily, there are no everyday concerns. There is no worry about a family, or about dry bread; there are no daily trifles and questions. Even the land he sees either dug up with trenches and craters, or covered with barbed wire. He has many leisure moments mentally, which are filled only with thoughts. Such bright, terrible, irreconcilable thoughts of freedom and death.

He is free—so everyone says, and indeed the whole arrangement of the army, so new and unusual, confirms this. But he must nevertheless go out to die and to kill—everyone says this too, even the committees chosen by him, even the delegates whom he sent to the congresses. But why die and kill? For the state, which up to this time had always been depicted to him as an evil, as the obligation to pay taxes, to be drafted, and whose creative role he in his dirty hovel never felt nor understood. For land and liberty? But what is the connection between the defense of Riga or the capture of Lvov and the land of the near-by landlord in Saratov Province? And besides perhaps he does not want either to die or to kill for these earthly goods.

Of course, the masses did not enunciate these thoughts so distinctly. They only hovered over them as a sort of murky mood and manifested themselves as a sort of passive disobedience to authority and commands. And here persuasion could not work. Command and compulsion were necessary. And for this was needed the determination to command and the opportunity to compel. . . .

Above all, the sharp turn in the direction of strong authority [after the July Days] met with a certain counter-action in the committees, especially in the 12th Army, where there was no master's hand like General Danilov's. The new word was too unfamiliar for the committeemen, accustomed to the benign phraseology of the early days of the revolution about conscious discipline, etc. The "Iskosol 12," as the executive committee of soldiers' deputies of the 12th Army was called for short, a heterogeneous body, and fiery sometimes to the point of hysterics, bristled every time we had to take decisive steps. True, there was no case when we did not succeed in persuading the committee—sometimes it changed its mind exactly 180 degrees. I remember an instance when the committee arranged a confrontation for Voytinsky[1] and me with representatives of the Bolshevik organizations in regard to the closing of the newspaper "Trench Pravda." The Bolsheviks, with the obvious sympathy of the presidium of the committee, began to argue that "Trench Pravda" had lately been conducting itself moderately and deserved mercy. I took the "model" numbers of "Pravda" they had brought and, reading some passages from the resolutions printed there, declared that the question should not be whether to permit the publication of "Trench Pravda," but only whether to bring its publishers before the military-revolutionary court on charges of disorganizational appeals. Voytinsky, still almost a Bolshevik by reputation, expressed himself no less sharply. Towards the end of the meeting the whole presidium—Kuchin, Kharash, and the others—indicated that they were on our side. But such persuasion required time, sometimes concessions and compromises. The affair did not reach the breaking point, but all the time there was a strain, and the committee several times produced resolutions about the necessity of re-

[1] [Commissar of the 12th Army, formerly a Bolshevik—ED.]

moving me from the front on account of insufficient respect for the representative institutions in the army. But each time the resolution remained under wraps. Perhaps this was because at the first visit of the committee I declared that I would work in the army only in consideration of the directives of the Government, but together with this, I would consider it impossible to remain at the front if the committee declared that it did not trust me.

Not only the committee but also the commanding staff, baffled by the revolution, did not know how to approach this firm authority which was spoken of so much in the rear. Kerensky in my presence decided to close "Trench Pravda" and sent a telegram to this effect to the 12th Army. But it appeared that "Trench Pravda" still continued to come out. Klembovsky[2] advised me that in the 12th Army they did not know how to approach the matter, and asked me to go myself and settle the matter. For my arrival in Riga the whole general staff, the chief of the garrison, the commander had gathered. Everyone represented it as definitely impossible to carry out the order, since this would evoke disorders, mutinies, etc. I had to simplify the question; not giving in to their prognosis regarding the future, I simply called attention to the fact that the order, evoked by the weightiest considerations, had been given, and therefore it must be carried out promptly. For the commanding staff such a posing of the question seemed most convincing, and in fact, the following day "Trench Pravda" was closed, without any excesses or misunderstandings. True, the Bolsheviks complained that our attitude toward them was not correct enough and tried to find support from me. But later they gave up even this hope. True, they quickly began to publish a new newspaper, "Trench Tocsin," but extraordinarily restrained and pale, even. But even here we did not avoid misunderstandings. On my second visit to Riga I purposely stopped by the office of "Trench Tocsin" and bought several sets to get acquainted with it. At headquarters the chief of staff had already begun to tell me with a secretive look that according to the information of his agents the Bolsheviks were publishing "Trench Tocsin" in place of "Trench Pravda," and that he hoped shortly to get a copy of this paper. Truly without any special feeling of triumph I showed him the five numbers I had just bought.

But it was especially difficult to take more decisive measures in what was then technically termed our "clean" army. Practically every division had its Bolshevik with a name better known in the army than the name of the division commander.

---

[2] [Commander of the Northern Front—Ed.]

Since it was clear that without removing them it would be impossible to deal with the dissolution of the army, we gradually got rid of one celebrity after another. But measures of arrest could naturally be taken only by the commander, since he was in charge of the military forces. Generals like Boldyrev were little disturbed by such tasks. The famous Captain Sivers, whose name resounded from the Baltic Sea to the Carpathians, was arrested surprisingly easily: under some pretext he was given an order to appear at headquarters; there they put him in a car and took him to jail. But in one of the divisions of the 6th Siberian Corps we got a different picture. The commander of the division took no precautions, and without having reliable forces ready, gave the order to make an arrest. The whole company to which the Bolshevik belonged became rebellious and firmly declared that it would not surrender "its own man," and the commander of the division did not have the forces at hand to compel this. The next day forces were readied to move against the company, and the order was repeated. But now the conflict involved the whole regiment, as the other companies united with the first. The following day they had to set up an expedition of all three kinds of arms. But while the units of the punitive detachment were getting hopelessly mixed up and failed to appear on time, the whole division came out for the rebels. Only thanks to the intervention of Voytinsky did they succeed in finding some kind of escape from the situation. Convinced that the punitive detachment could not be of any use, he went off to talk with the company, and, in spite of the terrible excitement of the soldiers, managed to have the arrested man sent to division headquarters. But the company, in turn, insisted on being at headquarters too. Thus, if one takes into account the fact that the headquarters guard consisted of eight men, it appeared that the division commander had not so much arrested the Bolshevik, as the Bolshevik had arrested the division commander. All this was so scandalous that Klembovsky asked me to go to Riga and have a look at what was going on there. I got to a meeting of the army commander, the division commander, and the army commissar. I insisted on the prompt withdrawal of the whole division from the front and the most severe punishment of those guilty. But General Parsky firmly declared that he considered this only an unpleasant incident that did not disturb the battle readiness of the division, which could remain at the front. I declared just as definitely that I recognized the full priority of his opinion. I remember that the window of the quarters opened onto a square with a Gothic cathedral. Surprised and taken aback, I turned away from the army commander and said to Voytinsky that I understood for the first time how foreign the sharp tense lines of the Gothic were to the Russian soul.

The Nationalities' Revolution

The disintegration of central authority under the Provisional Government played directly into the movement for autonomy among Russia's national minorities. By mid-1917 the larger and more self-conscious minority peoples of European Russia—particularly the Ukraine and Finland—were virtually asserting their independence. The following declarations are from Browder and Kerensky, *The Russian Provisional Government*, pp. 383–85 (the Ukraine) and pp. 344–47 (Finland).

a) *The Ukraine: First Universal Declaration of the Central Rada [Council], June 10, 1917*

People of the Ukraine, nation of peasants, workers, and toilers:

By your will you placed us, the Ukrainian Central Rada, as the guardians of the rights and freedoms of the Ukrainian land.

Your best sons, elected by people from the villages, from factories, from soldiers' barracks, from all the large bodies and groups in the Ukraine, have elected us, the Ukrainian Central Rada, and entrusted us to defend these rights and freedoms.

Your elected men expressed their will thus:

Let there be a free Ukraine. Without separating from all of Russia, without breaking away from the Russian State, let the Ukrainian people on their own territory have the right to manage their own life. Let a National Ukrainian Assembly (Sejm), elected by universal, equal, direct, and secret suffrage, establish order and a regime in the Ukraine. Only your Ukrainian assembly is to have the right to issue all laws which are to establish this regime.

Those laws which will establish the regime throughout the entire Russian State must be issued by the All-Russian Parliament.

No one knows better than we what we need and which laws are best for us. No one can know better than our peasants how to manage our own land. Therefore we desire that, after all lands throughout Russia are confiscated as national property, *pomeshchik* [landlord], state, crown, monastic, and other lands, when a law is passed about this in the Constituent Assembly, the right to have control of our Ukrainian lands, the right to use them, belongs to us, to our Ukrainian Assembly (Sejm).

Thus spoke those elected from the entire Ukrainian land.

Having spoken thus, they elected from their midst the Ukrainian Central Rada and told us to stand at the head of our people, to guard their rights, and to create a new order of a free autonomous Ukraine.

And we, the Ukrainian Central Rada, fulfilled the wish of our people; we took upon ourselves the heavy burden of building a new life, and we have launched upon this work.

We had hoped that the central Russian Provisional Government would lend us a hand in this work in order that, jointly with it, we the Ukrainian Central Rada might organize our land.

But the Russian Provisional Government rejected all of our demands; it refused the outstretched hand of the Ukrainian people.

We sent our delegates to Petrograd to present to the Russian Provisional Government our demands.

And the chief demands were as follows:

That the Russian government publicly, by a special act, declare that it is not against the national freedom of the Ukraine, against the right of the people to autonomy.

That the central Russian government have in its cabinet our commissar on Ukrainian affairs for all matters related to the Ukraine.

That local authority in the Ukraine be united in one representative from the central Russian government, that is, by a commissar in the Ukraine elected by us.

That a certain portion of money collected by the central treasury from our people be returned to us, the representatives of this people, for their national and cultural needs.

All these demands of ours the central Russian government rejected.

It did not wish to say whether or not it recognizes the right of our people to autonomy, the right to rule their own life. It evaded the answer and referred us to the forthcoming Constituent Assembly.

The central Russian government did not wish to have in its cabinet our commissar; it did not wish to build jointly with us a new regime.

Likewise it did not want to recognize a commissar for all of the Ukraine in order that we might, together with it, lead our land to organization and order.

And it refused to return the money collected from our land for the needs of our schools, culture, and organization.

And now, people of the Ukraine, we are forced to create our own destiny. We cannot allow our land to be ruined and to collapse. If the Russian Provisional Government cannot introduce order in our land, if it does not want to initiate with us a great work, we must undertake it ourselves. It is our duty to our region and to the people who dwell upon our land.

And therefore we, the Ukrainian Central Rada, publish this Universal to all of our people and declare that from now on we shall build our own life.

Therefore let each member of our nation, each citizen of a village or city know henceforth that the hour of great work has struck.

From this time on, each village, each volost [township], each board, whether city or zemstvo [provincial assembly], that defends the interests of the Ukrainian people must have the most intimate organizational relations with the Central Rada.

Wherever, for some reason, administrative authority remains in the hands of people hostile to Ukrainization, we prescribe that our citizens launch upon a broad and mighty [campaign of] organization and information of the people and, after that, [elect a new] administration.

In towns and those places where the Ukrainian population lives together with other nationalities, we suggest that our citizens immediately establish relations and understandings with the democracy of those nationalities and jointly with them begin preparations for a new and correct life.

The Central Rada expresses the hope that the non-Ukrainian peoples who live in our land will also be concerned about peace and order in our territory and during this trying time of national disorganization will, in the spirit of friendship, together with us begin the organization of autonomy in the Ukraine.

And after we complete this preparatory organizational work, we shall call representatives from all peoples of the Ukrainian land and will work out laws for her. Those laws, that entire order which we shall prepare, the All-Russian Constituent Assembly must approve by its law.

People of the Ukraine, your electoral organ, the Ukrainian Central Rada, faces a great and high wall which it must demolish in order to lead its people out upon the road of freedom.

We need strength for this. We need strong and brave hands. We need the people's hard work. And for the success of this work we need, first of all, great means (money). Up to this time the Ukrainian people have turned all of their means into the All-Russian central treasury. And the people themselves never had, and have not now, anything in return for it.

The Ukrainian Central Rada consequently orders all organized citizens of villages and towns, all Ukrainian public boards and institutions, beginning with the 1st of July, to tax the population with a special tax for their own affairs and accurately and immediately transmit this tax regularly to the treasury of the Ukrainian Rada.

Ukrainian people! Your future is in your own hands. In this hour of trial, of total disorder and collapse, prove by your unanimity and statesmanship that you, a nation of grain producers, can proudly and with dignity take your place as the equal of any organized powerful nation.

b) Finland: Law of the Sejm [Parliament] on the Supreme Power in Finland, July 5, 1917, and Address of the Sejm to the Provisional Government, July 12, 1917

It is hereby decreed: With the cessation of the rights of the monarch, in accordance with the decision of the Sejm of Finland, the following becomes effective:

Article 1. The Sejm of Finland alone decides, affirms, and decrees on the implementation of all Finnish laws, among them those dealing with finances, taxation, and customs.

The Sejm also decides definitely on all other Finnish affairs which were, in accordance with the statutes in force up to this time, subject to the decision of the Tsar-Emperor and the Grand Duke. The provisions of this law do not extend to matters of external policy or to military legislation and administration.

Article 2. The Sejm meets in regular session without special convocation and sets the time of closing of the session. Pending the publication of a new form of government in Finland, the Sejm exercises, in accordance with Article 18 of the Sejm statute, the right to decide on the conducting of new elections and the dissolution of the Sejm.

Article 3. The Sejm shall designate the executive power of Finland. The Supreme Executive Power is temporarily executed by the economic department of the Finnish Senate, whose members are appointed and dismissed by the Sejm.

To the Provisional Government of Russia: The Finnish Sejm, in accordance with the procedure for publishing the basic laws of the country, established by Article 60 of the Sejm statute, adopted and published on July 18 (new style) of this year the law attached herewith on the exercise of the supreme power in Finland. This law is based on the legal principle that with the deposition of the monarchy, the national representation of Finland has the right to enter upon the exercise of supreme state power on domestic matters of the country.

Thus the internal political freedom of Finland on the strength of clear law and right will rest upon a firm foundation of popular government and will depend upon the personal will of the Finnish people.

According to her constitution, Finland had been in the past also a free state in internal affairs, independent of Russian organs of administration and legislation, although in some local affairs authority belonged to Russia as well. However, Finland's right to internal independence was easily violated in practice as long as Russia was ruled by the Tsar, who was simultaneously also the monarch of Finland.

Juridically, as the monarch of Finland he exercised Finnish state authority and was bound by the Finnish fundamental laws. In practice, however, he not infrequently and systematically attempted to transfer the right of the Finnish monarch and even the right of the Finnish Senate to the government and legislative institutions of Russia.

The functions and democratic development of the Sejm were

suppressed, and, finally, the development of the entire legislation of the country was chained. Hanging over our people was the unbearable scourge of arbitrary rule, oppression, compulsory taxation, as well as hatred and grief. The lawful relations between Russia and Finland were turning into an enslavement of the Finnish people. The deposition of the monarchy by the Russian revolution saved Finland from this.

Moreover, it fell to the lot of the Finnish Sejm to protect and defend, in accordance with the fundamental laws, the rights of the supreme power of Finland, formerly belonging to the monarch, and the freedom of the country.

The Sejm could not, under the changed state of affairs, leave the government authority to Russia, because now, as before, this would be tantamount to limitation of the constituent rights of Finland and would be a serious undermining of the country's political position. The preservation of the internal independence of Finland called for the transfer of the supreme state power in internal matters of the country to the Finnish people in order that it be exercised by her own national organs and her highest instance, the popular representation.

The form of the country's government, operative since the period of Swedish rule, and the even more ancient legislation naturally do not give specific instructions with respect to the present state of affairs. But, in spite of their monarchical spirit, they do make provision for the independent power of the institution of national representation in those cases where the lawful monarch does not exist. In view of the fact that the exercise of the supreme power by Finland during the period of interregnum, which has reigned for the past few months, was not regulated by law, the administration of the most basic matters suffered greatly and could be exercised only with great effort.

However, the Sejm cherished the hope that the lawful conception of the right to self-determination of the Finnish people would soon awaken and find expression in the wide strata of the Russian people. Then the straightforward word was spoken by the revolutionary democracy of Russia. The All-Russian Congress of representatives of the Soviets of Workers' and Soldiers' Deputies expressed its willingness to support and demand the right of Finland's complete self-determination down to political independence. Thus, the Russian revolutionary democracy, itself intolerant of oppression, nobly took under its patronage the hopes of our people to achieve political independence.

However, this congress of representatives thought that the solution of the Finnish question in its entirety could be approved, on the part of Russia, only by the All-Russian Constituent Assembly. But for all immediate and practical purposes, while the congress of representatives enjoined the Provisional Government to take the necessary measures without delay for the realization of Finland's complete self-government, it demanded the recognition of the right of the Sejm to publish and finally approve all the laws dealing with Finland, except those concerning foreign relations and military legislation and administration; also to decide the questions on the convening and dissolution of the Sejm as well as recognition of Finland's right to decide independently upon its executive power. . . .

The Finnish Sejm does not wish to violate the rights of the Russian citizens and institutions now present in Finland. On the contrary, the Sejm intends to approve and implement at the earliest opportunity the laws that it adopted earlier and that extend to Russian citizens in Finland equal rights with those of the Finnish citizens, both civil and commercial, as well as laws abolishing the special restrictions now existing with respect to Jews.

Likewise the Sejm will see to it that the Russian citizens [residing] in Finland enjoy the right to freedom of unions, assembly, and speech without any obstacles. In the event of an actual need for a change in the status of Russians and of Russian institutions present in Finland, Finland will request permission for a preliminary conference with the government authority in Russia about them, as well as about the question of regulating mutual agreements on the manifold mutual economic relations between Russia and Finland.

Peaceful and free cooperation with the Russian people is an important condition for the prosperity of the Finnish people, and, firmly counting on the right-thinking Russian democracy, the Finnish Sejm cherishes the hope that the Provisional Government will find it possible to grant to Finland and her Sejm, in the name of Russia, the rights, established by law, to exercise supreme power in Finland.

The Peasants' Revolution

In the last analysis the most decisive force in the Russian Revolution was the upsurge of the peasants hungry for what was left of the landlords' estates. The Socialist Revolutionary, Victor Chernov, Minister of Agriculture in the Provisional Government from May to August, recounted in his memoirs his vain struggle to accomplish an orderly land reform and allay the upheaval in the countryside.

This excerpt is from Victor Chernov, *The Great Russian Revolution*, translated and abridged by Philip E. Mosely [copyright 1936, 1964] (New York: Russell & Russell, 1966), pp. 236–39, 242–44, 256–57, 259–63. (Reprinted by permission.)

Twenty-four commissions and subcommissions, under the Ministry of Agriculture, toiled ceaselessly, preparing for the Constituent Assembly a detailed plan of land reform and land organization. The work of these commissions, rudely interrupted by the October Revolution and completely abandoned, was later consulted frequently by the legislators and agrarian organizers of the Bolshevist Revolution. But they neglected its underlying purpose, the logical connection of its separate parts as elements of a single plan, calculated for at least a decade.

The Chief Land Committee and the Ministry of Agriculture were everywhere in close contact with the local population. They could not confine themselves to the academic work of planning the new agrarian order. Day-to-day existence brought its own burning problems, requirements, and conflicts. The village's most urgent needs had to be satisfied while leaving freedom of action to the future Constituent Assembly.

On the eve of the first session of the Chief Land Committee, on May 17, the Social Revolutionary Minister of Justice, Pereverzev, with Chernov telegraphed an administrative order to all notarial bureaus, stopping all dealings in land. But rumors spread persistently that on May 25 he had canceled that order under pressure by the majority in the Provisional Government. On June 1 the question of "measures to preserve the land supply intact till the general solution of the land question by the Constituent Assembly" was referred to a conference of representatives of four ministries, the

Land Banks, the mutual credit associations, and cooperatives. There it was pigeonholed. On June 7 a new telegram of the Minister of Justice removed all prohibition from tax contracts, purchases of nonagricultural land, and several other classes of contracts; on June 23 he ordered "the circular instructions concerning land contracts repealed." This was a course of "zigzags." On June 29 Chernov succeeded in putting through a law to wipe out the Stolypin land reform.[1] Immediately afterwards he suffered two serious defeats. The Provisional Government rejected a bill approved by the Chief Land Committee, on the use of meadow lands. This bill was to protect the interests of the peasantry which, at the emancipation of 1861, had been deprived of its due share of meadow lands; it transferred excess meadow land to the state. The cabinet rejected another bill to regulate fisheries through mediation by the Land Committees; private monopolies and fisheries contractors had encroached on the interests of fishermen and consumers.

Obviously, the same fate menaced all other bills, particularly that regulating rental relationships and utilization of forests. Diametrical opposition developed between the viewpoints of the Ministry of Internal Affairs and the Ministry of Agriculture. On June 11 Prince Lvov made a special report to the government on the mass of "revolutionary" decrees issued by local organs of popular government, in violation of the lawful rights of the landowners. He proposed that such decrees be declared invalid, and especially urged the necessity of a public declaration to this effect, signed jointly by himself and Chernov. The latter refused categorically, for the lack of new agrarian laws from above made "separate legislation" from below inevitable. Despite the imperfections of local legislation it was a lesser evil than efforts to compel the people to abide by the old Tsarist land laws, efforts which could end only in agrarian disorder and anarchy.

The idea of sabotage, of refusing to sow their fields, had become popular among a part of the landowners at the beginning of the revolution. In many places relations between peasants and landlords had now become so tense that the gentry could only abandon farming and passively watch it die. The Land Committees could no longer remain mere on-lookers. In Ranenburg district, Riazan province, a center of the more obstinate landlords, resolutions of village and county assemblies favoring abolition of rent contracts

[1] [The laws of 1909–11 permitting individual peasants to leave their commune and receive a compact farm—ED.]

and the "black partition" [2] compelled the Land Committee "to undertake to regulate this question." At a meeting of specially invited landowners, "influenced by the frightful impression caused by loss of almost two million poods of wheat on their estates, by the empty fields, by scraggly cattle lying in courtyards and dying on many estates," the committee made a radical decision. Part of the estates it resolved to take under its direct control, part to divide up for provisional use by the peasants. This decree and the following compromise decree were canceled by higher authority. Everything went back to the original state, with one result: "plowing was broken off."

The second plenary session of the Chief Land Committee met from July 1 to 6. The Mogilev delegate reported that "throughout the province proclamations were pasted up, signed by two princes, Lvov and Drutsky-Sokolinsky, who threatened severe punishment to all violators of the old land order." This made the peasants ask if the revolution had really happened, if it was not a dream. The representative of Kursk province reported that the provincial Land Committees were forced to work under terrible conditions. They were to bring order into land relationships, eliminate disorder and anarchy, but were not given money for travel expense. A simple resolution was ripening in the peasants' minds: "We will not give the landlord a single kopeck of rent in the district, but will turn all this money into the fund of the Land Committee." The Ministry of the Interior refused to countenance far less serious steps. When the Bogoroditsky district Executive Committee taxed the gentry's land equally with the peasants', the Ministry of the Interior denounced it as "arbitrary action"; it suggested that, in case of a deficiency in funds for the land agencies, the peasants might take up a collection. Encouraged by this support, the landlords in some places refused to pay local levies; then, as in Lifland, the county committees inventoried and auctioned their property. Everywhere attempts of the Land Committees to regulate rental relationships and rates met with threats of court action. The provinces vociferously demanded the new laws promised by the Provisional Government; the Minister of Agriculture could only reply that "the bills presented to the Provisional Government did not meet with unanimous approval." . . .

Chernov's bills did not attempt to force land relationships back

[2] [A traditional peasant goal of dividing up land retained by the landlords since 1861—ED.]

into the *old* channel. On the contrary, they openly favored the peasants' irresistible striving for the land, the right to which belonged solely to labor, in the popular conception of right. Chernov felt that the only way in which the agrarian legislator could escape "confirming an accomplished fact," whatever form it might take, was through legislation which would not always lag behind reality, as it had so far, but would hastily dig a new channel for its irresistible current.

Lvov's withdrawal from the ministry merely made a place at the head of the government for Kerensky, and in this conflict he was for the first and last time on Chernov's side. Utilizing the simultaneous resignation of the Kadet ministers over the Ukrainian question, and pressing home his advantage, Chernov finally put through his legislation forbidding dealings in land until the meeting of the Constituent Assembly. The only concession which he had to make was to substitute for the prohibitive form of the law an outwardly mild and permissive one: land contracts required in each case special permission of the local provincial Land Committee and confirmation by the Minister of Agriculture. In the Soviet of Peasants' Deputies and the All-Russian Central Executive Committee of Soviets, Chernov received noisy ovations. The policy of inaction, of helpless attempts to hem the peasantry within the framework of the prerevolutionary land code, seemed ended once and forever.

This hopeful feeling was jarred by a sharp dissonance. The commander of the Southwest front, General Kornilov, had issued an order for the entire frontal area on July 8; under pain of criminal prosecution and loss of property rights and arrest, he forbade all "arbitrary interference" in land relationships by local agencies. The order particularly prohibited compelling the gentry to raise the wages of war prisoners or removing these prisoners from the large estates to work for the soldiers' wives. The order provoked a ferment in both village and army. The general was not joking. The Poltava provincial land commissar was indicted for violating these decrees. The military authorities ordered such cases examined without delay; if necessary, military force was to be used. Emboldened by this example, civilian justice, represented by the state's attorney's offices, became active outside the frontal area. They began to arrest members of the Land Committees. The latter lost all authority among the population, and their further activity became impossible.

Chernov took a new step: On July 16 he issued "instructions to the Land Committees." He confirmed the right of the Land Committees to take over land which the landowners were unable to cultivate, and to distribute it among the peasants. He confirmed the power of the local Land Committees as mediators in revising rental contracts between owners and lessors. Peasants in a privileged situation, after deducting normal feed requirements for their own cattle, were to surrender the rest for war needs at fixed prices. The instruction permitted compulsory utilization of the gentry's animal and mechanical equipment, but required consent by Land and Supply Committees and direct supervision by them. The Land Committees were to supervise protection of forests against predatory lumbering and to secure for the peasants the privilege of taking wood for the actual needs of their households and for public institutions. Protection of model farms, blooded cattle and valuable crops was provided for. In conclusion, the instruction recommended that the Land Committees go half way to satisfy the just and well-founded demands of the toiling peasantry, that they regard themselves as the authorized organs of the state and count on the full support of the Ministry of Agriculture; the latter, in turn, would do everything it could to issue new laws, in order to "end the present precarious and indefinite situation in land relationships, the cause of similar precariousness and indefiniteness in the popular conception of right and law."

The Ministry of Agriculture was at once attacked by the Ministry of Justice: "The application of Sect. 4, Art. 7 of the decree on Land Committees, because of the right granted to Land Committees of issuing obligatory decrees affecting agricultural and land relationships, would mean limiting the right to dispose of private property."

It is hard to believe that such a view could be proclaimed, not in the revolution, but even during the World War, which had long since made private property a social function, hemmed in by a multitude of limitations and instructions, beneath the Damocles' sword of requisition. . . .

At the second session of the Chief Land Committee the representative of Nizhni-Novgorod province reported that there was only one topic among the peasants: "We are tired of waiting, we have waited three hundred years, and now that we have conquered power, we do not want to wait any more."

What were they waiting for? They were told: For the Constituent Assembly. Unfortunately, this assembly was postponed with depressing regularity. No better means for sickening the peasant of the Constituent Assembly could have been invented.

And so the idea that there was no need to wait for the Constituent Assembly and that the land must be seized at once found ready soil. At the second session of the Chief Land Committee a Smolensk representative reported the talk of the peasants in Sychevsky district: "They say of the Constituent Assembly: Well, Nicholas was overthrown without the Constituent Assembly; why can't the gentry be driven from the face of the earth without it?" The Bolsheviks, who were on the job, nudged them: They can be. You have only to set up a workers' and peasants' dictatorship and settle all problems "in two shakes of a lamb's tail," with a mere flourish of the pen at the foot of revolutionary decrees.

The gentry were not at all scared by this. Dictatorship, Bolshevism, what difference to them if the Constituent Assembly would not leave them their land, or pay them for it? The "worse, the better"— let everything be done in the most abrupt and despotic way. On this *reductio ad absurdum* the revolution would break its own neck.

Later even a progressive and cautious landlord and Octobrist, Shidlovsky, wrote:

> I think that the Bolsheviks, without suspecting it, did Russia a colossal service, an unforgettable service, in dispersing the Constituent Assembly, presided over by Chernov. Nothing good could come from it, while it would have done no less harm than the Bolsheviks, though without dictatorship or terrorism; I feel that if the country was doomed to experience a severe crisis, it is better to have all the scorpions at once than gradually.

If people could say this after having experienced the scourges of dictatorship and terrorism, it was all the easier for them to uphold this "negative Maximalism" when the "dictatorship of the proletariat" was merely a vague, abstract idea, which had not yet revealed its contents of blood and terror. . . .

The gentry could now only try to postpone as long as possible the convocation of the Constituent Assembly, and meanwhile squeeze all they could from their estates. The estates could be mortgaged and remortgaged, thus gaining for their owners far more than by government compensation. The "cream could be skimmed" by cutting down the valuable forests and selling off the best animal and mechanical equipment. Parceling, real or fictitious, could be resorted to in order to conceal a surplus of land over and above the norm guaranteed against confiscation. Land could be sold to foreigners whose property rights would be defended by their governments. Unbridled land speculation was rife.

The peasantry at once sensed the new menace. "Beware the

masters do not twist us around their finger again," "Be careful not
to let the land slip," was heard everywhere. The first and universal
demand of the village was now the prohibition of all contracts of
sale, mortgage, donation, etc., until the meeting of the Constituent
Assembly; secondly, to avoid this partial decline, the estates, with
all their stock, equipment, meadows, etc., must be taken under the
control of the local Land Committees. This added a new dispute to
the quarrels about rentals, prisoners of war, wages on the estates,
use of hay fields, forests. It implied constant invasion of the noble's
farmyard by the peasant. Had the owner sent the blooded cattle
away? Were the rumors true about his mortgaging the land or
selling the forest? Regarding the noble's estate as the lawful heritage
of the emancipated people, the village set up its own guardianship
over it. Where the nobles consented, peaceful and even neighborly
relations were restored. Where the gentry resisted—and where did
they not resist?—their Maximalism provoked the gloomy counter-
Maximalism of the peasants.

The soil was prepared for Bolshevism. It began to penetrate,
taking on a primitive aspect in a primitive environment.

A Bolshevist peasant describes the birth of village Bolshevism in
Tambov province:

> At the meeting the peasants split into two groups. One proposed
> to take the estates from the nobles in an orderly way and divide up
> all the property proportionately among the population, but to pre-
> serve the gentry's buildings for cultural purposes. The other group
> proposed to burn down all the estates immediately, not leaving one
> stone on another; "by orderliness," they said, "we shall never drive
> the nobles from the estates."
>
> The poor peasants favored the second group, the proletarians, and
> they were the majority. At exactly ten in the evening the crowd, feel-
> ing its gigantic power, approached Romanov's estate. They broke
> into the house, dragged the owner out to the street in only his night-
> gown, and the vengeance began. . . . They set fire to the wheat and
> the estate, and began to plunder the house.
>
> The fiery signal was caught up by other villages: the peasants of
> Yaroslavka went to plunder and burn the Davydov estate, the peasants
> of Tidvorka and Yekaterinino burned the Ushakovs' estate, and
> Komarov's, the village of Bashovo burned Volosatova-Zaeva, and dur-
> ing the night of September 7–8 a sea of conflagrations swept over the
> estates of our country. On the morning of September 8 along the
> road to the village crowds of people were straggling with stolen prop-
> erty: some with wheat, others with a bed, cattle, or a broken arm-
> chair.

In Chernigov province, on the estate of the former president of the nobility, Sudienko, "the stock, equipment, furniture, etc., were divided by the peasants, each taking whatever he could. The land was divided among the peasants, and all the buildings burned down. In the mansion house there were many historical treasures, and an enormous library, which the peasants tore up to roll cigarettes. Paintings by famous artists were torn off before the house was burned and used to make trousers. . . ."

The nobles did not want "Chernov's partition" at any cost. They preferred the "black partition" and they had their "black partition." [3]

Oh, yes, they thought it would turn out differently. They thought that the peasantry's rushing headlong into wild excesses would help serve to rouse the Provisional Government from its irresolution and lead it to send military detachments to subdue the peasants.

That was stark madness. There was no better means of demoralizing the army than to send it, with its 90% of peasants, to crush the movement of millions of its brethren.

In Samara province the soldiers' wives raised a rebellion:

> Let us go and mow the grass of the gentry; why are our husbands suffering for the third year? The gentry brought a detachment of soldiers from Hvalynsk. But when the soldiers, who were peasants themselves, saw the muzhiks mowing the rich grass, they tried their hand at mowing; they were tired of their rifles. The peasants fed the soldiers, talked to them, and then set to work all the harder.

In Tambov province a military detachment came at the summons of Prince Viazemsky. It was greeted by a roar from the crowd: "What are you doing, coming to defend the prince, coming to beat your own fathers? Throw the devils into the river!" The commander took it into his head to fire into the air. He was struck by a stone and ordered the troops to disperse the mob, but the soldiers did not stir. The officer spurred his horse and escaped from the enraged peasants by fording the river. His detachment scattered and let the crowd surround the prince, whom they arrested and sent to the front as a "slacker." At a near-by station he was lynched by a detachment of Siberian shock troops on their way to the front.

In Slavuta, Iziaslavsky district, Volhynia province, a detachment of fifty Cossacks was sent to the Sangushko estate to pacify the

---

[3] [In the original Russian this is a pun on Chernov's name, the equivalent of "Mr. Black"—ED.]

peasants. A detachment of infantry from the front was also quartered nearby. The Cossacks went out to reconnoiter in the woods. The soldiers then "set out with the peasants. First, they burst into the prince's palace. The prince tried to flee. The soldiers quickly scattered to search for him. They overtook him near a steep bridge and tossed him on their bayonets; three times they lifted Sangushko on their bayonets, at the fourth thrust the bayonet went straight to his heart. The soldiers and peasants, without wasting time, carried three iron chests from the mansion, with several million rubles in gold, silver, and paper money, distributed the money to the poor, and then burned the chambers of the prince. The peasants went boldly out to divide the land, afraid of no one."

Gray-uniformed peasants, aroused by the revolution in the city, were sent against the village, which would not and could not go on indefinitely under the Tsarist agrarian laws, once Tsarism had fallen. A more suicidal policy could not have been invented.

Part Four

🎜 THE BOLSHEVIKS
PREPARE

By the fall of 1917, with the rising tide of popular unrest, the worsening divisions in the Provisional Government, and the momentary disrepute of the Right in the aftermath of the Kornilov adventure, the stage was set for the new revolution Lenin had called for. The Petrograd and Moscow Soviets, subject to changing composition as deputies were recalled by their constituents and replaced with more radical individuals, came under Bolshevik control early in September, and Trotsky was elected chairman of the Petrograd Soviet. Lenin began to issue a stream of written orders from his hideout in Finland to the Bolshevik Central Committee in Petrograd urging preparations for the armed seizure of power by the Bolshevik Party.

From this point on the history of the Revolution took a path that was as unlikely as it was complicated. The Bolshevik leadership in the main resisted Lenin's demand for armed insurrection as a course of unnecessary risk, and chose instead to wait for the Second All-Russian Congress of Soviets, scheduled for October 20, as an opportunity to be voted into power. Still under threat of arrest, Lenin secretly went to Petrograd early in October to impress his line of forceful action on his apprehensive followers, and got the nominal assent of a majority at the Central Committee meetings of October 10 and 16. Only his old lieutenants Zinoviev and Kamenev voiced open opposition. Nevertheless, Bolshevik efforts to organize the Petrograd garrison through the Military Revolutionary Committee of the Soviet were slow and defensively oriented— the main concern was to guard the Congress of Soviets against a new Kornilov-type coup. Even with the postponement of the Congress five days by the moderate Socialists, the Bolsheviks had no detailed preparations ready for offensive action until fighting broke out on October 24, the day before the Congress actually opened.

Lenin Calls for Insurrection

Observing the rise of the revolutionary fever from his hiding place in Helsinki (then Helsingfors), Lenin addressed two letters to the Bolshevik Central Committee between September 12 and 14 (the first of which is given here in full) demanding the immediate preparation of an armed uprising. The Central Committee, expecting victory through mass agitation, was "bewildered," according to one participant, and decided to ignore the directive. Lenin pursued his aim with a series of letters and articles, notably "The Crisis Has Matured," in which he analyzed Russian events in relation to the anticipated world revolution and threatened to resign if his wishes were not heeded.

The English translations which follow are from V. I. Lenin, *Collected Works* (Moscow: Progress Publishers, 1964), 26:19–21, 74, 77, 82–85.

The Bolsheviks Must Assume Power

A Letter to the Central Committee and the Petrograd and Moscow Committees of the R.S.D.W.P.(B.)

The Bolsheviks, having obtained a majority in the Soviets of Workers' and Soldiers' Deputies of both capitals, can and *must* take state power into their own hands.

They can because the active majority of revolutionary elements in the two chief cities is large enough to carry the people with it, to overcome the opponent's resistance, to smash him, and to gain and retain power. For the Bolsheviks, by immediately proposing a democratic peace, by immediately giving the land to the peasants and by reestablishing the democratic institutions and liberties which have been mangled and shattered by Kerensky, will form a government which *nobody* will be able to overthrow.

The majority of the people are *on our side*. This was proved by the long and painful course of events from May 6 to August 31 and to September 12. The majority gained in the Soviets of the metropolitan cities *resulted* from the people coming over *to our side*. The wavering of the Socialist-Revolutionaries and Mensheviks and the increase in the number of internationalists within their ranks prove the same thing.

The Democratic Conference represents *not* a majority of the revolutionary people, but *only the compromising upper strata of the petty bourgeoisie*. We must not be deceived by the election figures; elections prove nothing. Compare the elections to the city councils of Petrograd and Moscow with the elections to the Soviets. Compare the elections in Moscow with the Moscow strike of August 12. Those are objective facts regarding that majority of revolutionary elements that are leading the people.

The Democratic Conference is deceiving the peasants; it is giving them neither peace nor land.

A Bolshevik government *alone* will satisfy the demands of the peasants.

Why must the Bolsheviks assume power at this very *moment?*

Because the impending surrender of Petrograd will make our chances a hundred times less favourable.

And it is *not in our power* to prevent the surrender of Petrograd while the army is headed by Kerensky and Co.

Nor can we "wait" for the Constituent Assembly, for by surrendering Petrograd Kerensky and Co. *can* always *frustrate* its convocation. Our Party alone, on taking power, can secure the Constituent Assembly's convocation; it will then accuse the other parties of procrastination and will be able to substantiate its accusations.

A separate peace between the British and German imperialists must and can be prevented, but only by quick action.

The people are tired of the waverings of the Mensheviks and Socialist-Revolutionaries. It is only our victory in the metropolitan cities that will carry the peasants with us.

We are concerned now not with the "day," or "moment" of insurrection in the narrow sense of the word. That will be only decided by the common voice of those who are *in contact* with the workers and soldiers, with *the masses*.

The point is that now, at the Democratic Conference, our Party has virtually *its own congress,* and this congress (whether it wishes to or not) *must* decide the *fate of the revolution.*

The point is to make the *task* clear to the Party. The present task must be an *armed uprising* in Petrograd and Moscow (with its region), the seizing of power and the overthrow of the government. We must consider *how* to agitate for this without expressly saying as much in the press.

We must remember and weigh Marx's words about insurrection, *"Insurrection is an art,"* etc.

It would be naive to wait for a "formal" majority for the Bolsheviks. No revolution ever waits for *that.* Kerensky and Co. are not waiting either, and are preparing to surrender Petrograd. It is the wretched waverings of the Democratic Conference that are bound to exhaust the patience of the workers of Petrograd and Moscow! History will not forgive us if we do not assume power now.

There is no apparatus? There is an apparatus—the Soviets and the democratic organisations. The international situation *right* now, on *the eve* of the conclusion of a separate peace between the British and the Germans, is *in our favour.* To propose peace to the nations right now means *to win.*

By taking power both in Moscow and in Petrograd *at once* (it doesn't matter which comes first, Moscow may possibly begin), we shall win *absolutely and unquestionably.*

N. Lenin

The Crisis Has Matured

The end of September undoubtedly marked a great turning-point in the history of the Russian revolution and, to all appearances, of the world revolution as well.

The world working-class revolution began with the action of individuals, whose boundless courage represented everything honest that remained of that decayed official "socialism" which is in reality social-chauvinism. Liebknecht in Germany, Adler in Austria, Mac-

Lean in Britain—these are the best-known names of the isolated heroes who have taken upon themselves the arduous role of fore-runners of the world revolution.

The second stage in the historical preparation for this revolution was a widespread mass discontent, expressing itself in the split of the official parties, in illegal publications and in street demonstrations. The protest against the war became stronger, and the number of victims of government persecution increased. The prisons of countries famed for their observance of law and even for their freedom—Germany, France, Italy and Britain—became filled with tens and hundreds of internationalists, opponents of the war and advocates of a working-class revolution.

The third stage has now begun. This stage may be called the eve of revolution. Mass arrests of party leaders in free Italy, and particularly the beginning of *mutinies* in the German army, are indisputable symptoms that a great turning-point is at hand, that we are *on the eve of a world-wide revolution.*

Even before this there were, no doubt, individual cases of mutiny among the troops in Germany, but they were so small, so weak and isolated that it was possible to hush them up—and that was the chief way of checking the *mass contagion* of seditious action. Finally, there developed such a movement in the navy that it was *impossible* to hush it up, despite all the severity of the German regime of military servitude, severity elaborated with amazing minuteness of detail and observed with incredible pedantry.

Doubt is out of the question. We are on the threshold of a world proletarian revolution. And since of all the proletarian internationalists in all countries only we Russian Bolsheviks enjoy a measure of freedom—we have a legal party and a score or so of papers, we have the Soviets of Workers' and Soldiers' Deputies of both capitals on our side, and we have the support of a *majority* of the people in a time of revolution—to us the saying, "To whom much has been given, of him much shall be required" in all justice can and must be applied. . . .

What, then, is to be done? We must *aussprechen was ist,* "state the facts," admit the truth that there is a tendency, or an opinion, in our Central Committee and among the leaders of our Party which favours *waiting* for the Congress of Soviets, and is *opposed* to taking power immediately, is *opposed* to an immediate insurrection. That tendency, or opinion, must be *overcome.*

Otherwise, the Bolsheviks will cover themselves with eternal *shame* and *destroy themselves* as a party.

For to miss such a moment and to "wait" for the Congress of Soviets would be *utter idiocy, or sheer treachery.*

It would be sheer treachery to the German workers. Surely we should not wait until their revolution *begins.* In that case even the Lieberdans[1] would be in favour of "supporting" it. But it *cannot* begin as long as Kerensky, Kishkin[2] and Co. are in power.

It would be sheer treachery to the peasants. To allow the peasant revolt to be suppressed when we control the Soviets of both *capitals* would be to *lose, and justly lose,* every ounce of the peasants' confidence. In the eyes of the peasants we would be putting ourselves on a level with the Lieberdans and other scoundrels.

To "wait" for the Congress of Soviets would be utter idiocy, for it would mean losing *weeks* at a time when weeks and even days decide *everything.* It would mean faint-heartedly *renouncing* power, for on November 1–2 it will have become impossible to take power (both politically and technically, since the Cossacks would be mobilised for the day of the insurrection so foolishly "appointed").

To "wait" for the Congress of Soviets is idiocy, for the Congress will *give nothing, and can give nothing!*

"Moral" importance? Strange indeed, to talk of the "importance" of resolutions and conversations with the Lieberdans when we know that the Soviets *support* the peasants and that the peasant revolt is *being suppressed!* We would be reducing the *Soviets* to the status of wretched debating parlours. First defeat Kerensky, then call the Congress.

The Bolsheviks are now *guaranteed* the success of the insurrection: (1) we can (if we do not "wait" for the Soviet Congress) launch a *surprise* attack from three points—from Petrograd, from Moscow and from the Baltic fleet; (2) we have slogans that guarantee us support—down with the government that is suppressing the revolt of the peasants against the landowners! (3) we have a majority *in the country;* (4) the disorganisation among the Mensheviks and the Socialist-Revolutionaries is complete; (5) we are technically in a position to take power in Moscow (where the start might even be made, so as to catch the enemy unawares); (6) we have *thousands* of armed workers and soldiers in Petrograd who could *at once* seize the Winter Palace, the General Staff building, the telephone exchange

---

[1] [A play on the names of the Menshevik leaders Lieber and Dan—ED.]
[2] [The Kadet Minister of Welfare—ED.]

and the large printing presses. Nothing will be able to drive us out, while agitational work in the *army* will be such as to make it *impossible* to combat this government of peace, of land for the peasants, and so forth.

If we were to attack at once, suddenly, from three points, Petrograd, Moscow and the Baltic fleet, the chances are a hundred to one that we would succeed with smaller sacrifices than on July 3–5, because *the troops will not advance* against a government of peace. Even though Kerensky *already* has "loyal" cavalry, etc., in Petrograd, if we were to attack from two sides, he would be compelled to *surrender* since *we* enjoy the sympathy of the army. If with such chances as we have at present we do not take power, then all talk of transferring the power to the Soviets becomes *a lie.*

To refrain from taking power now, to "wait," to indulge in talk in the Central Executive Committee, to confine ourselves to "fighting for the organ" (of the Soviet), "fighting for the Congress," is *to doom the revolution to failure.*

In view of the fact that the Central Committee has *even left unanswered* the persistent demands I have been making for such a policy ever since the beginning of the Democratic Conference, in view of the fact that the Central Organ is *deleting* from my articles all references to such glaring errors on the part of the Bolsheviks as the shameful decision to participate in the Pre-parliament, the admission of Mensheviks to the Presidium of the Soviet, etc., etc.—I am compelled to regard this as a "subtle" hint at the unwillingness of the Central Committee even to consider this question, a subtle hint that I should keep my mouth shut, and as a proposal for me to retire.

I am compelled to *tender my resignation from the Central Committee,* which I hereby do, reserving for myself freedom to campaign among the *rank and file* of the Party and at the Party Congress.

For it is my profound conviction that if we "wait" for the Congress of Soviets and let the present moment pass, we shall *ruin* the revolution.

N. LENIN

September 29.

P. S. There are a number of facts which serve to prove that *even* the Cossack troops will not go against a government of peace! And how many are there? Where are they? And will not the entire army dispatch units *for our support?*

The Central Committee's Decision

On or before October 7 (the date is disputed among Soviet authorities) Lenin rode the train into Petrograd disguised as the locomotive fireman, and on the 10th met his Central Committee for the first time since the July Days. After an all-night argument, the group acceded in principle to Lenin's insistence on a program of armed insurrection prior to the scheduled Congress of Soviets. Lenin's resolution was adopted by a vote of 10 to 2 (Zinoviev and Kamenev). (Translated in Lenin, *Collected Works*, 26:190.)

The Central Committee recognises that the international position of the Russian revolution (the revolt in the German navy which is an extreme manifestation of the growth throughout Europe of the world socialist revolution; the threat of peace by the imperialists with the object of strangling the revolution in Russia) as well as the military situation (the indubitable decision of the Russian bourgeoisie and Kerensky and Co. to surrender Petrograd to the Germans), and the fact that the proletarian party has gained a majority in the Soviets—all this, taken in conjunction with the peasant revolt and the swing of popular confidence towards our Party (the elections in Moscow), and, finally, the obvious preparations being made for a second Kornilov revolt (the withdrawal of troops from Petrograd, the dispatch of Cossacks to Petrograd, the encircling of Minsk by Cossacks, etc.)—all this places the armed uprising on the order of the day.

Considering therefore that an armed uprising is inevitable, and that the time for it is fully ripe, the Central Committee instructs all Party organisations to be guided accordingly, and to discuss and decide all practical questions (the Congress of Soviets of the Northern Region, the withdrawal of troops from Petrograd, the action of our people in Moscow and Minsk, etc.) from this point of view.

The Opposition of Zinoviev and Kamenev

Following the Central Committee vote of October 10 in favor of insurrection, Zinoviev and Kamenev composed a letter protesting the decision as a dangerous risk, and circulated it to the principal Bolshevik Party committees. Press reports about the letter the following week were the occasion of Lenin's denunciation of Zinoviev and Kamenev for "strike-breaking."

The Zinoviev-Kamenev letter was published as an appendix in V. I. Lenin, *Sochineniya* [Works], 2nd ed. (Moscow and Leningrad: State Press, 1929), 21:495–97. (Editor's translation.)

A tendency is accumulating and growing in workers' circles that sees the only way out in immediately proclaiming an armed uprising. All due dates have now converged, such that if one speaks of such an uprising, he has to set the time openly, and in the next few days. In one form or another this question is already being discussed by the whole periodical press, and in workers' meetings, and it occupies the minds of a considerable circle of party workers. We, in turn, consider it our duty and our right to express ourselves on this question with full frankness.

We are most deeply convinced that to proclaim an armed uprising right now means to gamble not only the fate of our party but the fate of the Russian and international revolution as well.

There is no doubt that there occur such historical situations where the oppressed class has to recognize that it is better to go down to defeat than to surrender without a fight. Does the Russian working class now find itself in such a situation? *No, a thousand times no!!!* . . .

As a result of the tremendous growth of the influence of our party in the cities and especially in the army, such a situation has shaped up at the present time that it is becoming a more and more impossible thing for the bourgeoisie to disrupt the Constituent Assembly. Through the army, through the workers we hold a revolver at the temple of the bourgeoisie: the bourgeoisie is put in such a position that if it thought of making an attempt to disrupt the Constituent Assembly now, it would again push the petty-bourgeois parties toward us, and the hammer of the revolver would be released.

The chances of our party in the elections to the Constituent Assembly are excellent. We believe that the talk that the influence of the Bolsheviks is beginning to fall is emphatically without foundation. In the mouths of our political opponents this assertion is simply a maneuver in a political game that counts precisely on evoking a move by the Bolsheviks under conditions favorable to our enemies. The influence of the Bolsheviks is growing. Whole strata of the toiling population have just begun to be caught up by it. With the correct tactics we can win a third or even more of the seats in the Constituent Assembly. The position of the petty-bourgeois parties in the Constituent Assembly cannot be entirely the same as it is right now. Above all, their slogan, "For land, for freedom, wait for the Constituent Assembly," will be dropped. And the intensification of poverty, hunger, and the peasant movement will put more and more pressure on them and compel them to seek an alliance with the proletarian party against the landlords and capitalists represented by the Kadet Party. . . .

In Russia the majority of the workers and a significant part of the soldiers are for us. But all the rest is questionable. We are all convinced, for instance, that if the matter now reaches the point of the elections to the Constituent Assembly, the peasants will vote in the majority for the S.-R.'s. What is this—an accident? The mass of the soldiers supports us not because of the slogan of war, but because of the slogan of peace. This is an extremely important circumstance, failing to consider which we risk building all our calculations on sand. If we now take power alone and confront (as a result of the whole world situation) the necessity of waging revolutionary war, the mass of the soldiers will pour away from us. . . .

And here we approach the second assertion—that the international proletariat is supposedly now already with us, in the majority. This unfortunately is not yet so. The mutiny in the German navy has an immense symptomatic significance. The harbingers of a serious movement are present in Italy. But from this it is still very far to any amount of active support for the proletarian revolution in Russia, declaring war on the whole bourgeois world. It is extremely bad to overestimate one's forces. Undoubtedly much has been given to us and much will be asked of us. But if we now stake the whole game on one card and suffer a defeat—we will deal a cruel blow as well to the international proletarian revolution, which is growing very slowly but nevertheless growing. In time the growth of the revolution in Europe would make it obligatory for us to take power in our hands immediately, without any hesitation. In this consists the sole guarantee of the victoriousness of an uprising of the proletariat in Russia. This will come, but it is not yet. . . .

Before history, before the international proletariat, before the Russian Revolution and the Russian working class we do not now have the right to stake the whole future on the card of an armed uprising. It would be a mistake to think that a move now similar to that of July 3–5 would in the event of failure lead only to such consequences. Now the question is bigger. The question is decisive battle, and defeat in *this* battle would be defeat for the revolution.

Hesitation in the Bolshevik Ranks

A secret session of the Petrograd City Committee on October 15 heard an extended debate about the state of preparations for an armed uprising. The minutes were published in *Krasnaya letopis* [The Red Chronicle], no. 2–3, 1922, pp. 324–32. The following translation is reprinted from James Bunyan and H. H. Fisher, eds., *The Bolshevik Revolution, 1917–1918* (Stanford, Calif.: Stanford University Press, 1934), pp. 69–74. (Copyright 1934 by the Board of Trustees of the Leland Stanford Junior University. Copyright renewed 1961 by James Bunyan and H. H. Fisher. This and the following selections from this volume reprinted with the permission of the publishers.)

Comrade Bubnov made [*the following*] *report:* At the present moment the whole situation may be summed up as follows: We are approaching a climax, the crisis has fully developed, and events are beginning to unfold themselves. We are being drawn into a struggle with forces directed against us. We are on the eve of an insurrection. Rodzianko claims that he will surrender Petersburg in order to strangle the revolution. Everything is against us. Kerensky is bringing into play diplomatic cunning; he is attempting to remove the troops from Petersburg. . . . Six months of the revolution have brought us to the brink of ruin. As a consequence the masses are beginning to denounce everybody and everything. We must give this situation our most concentrated attention. In order to organize these elementary forces and to save the revolution we must take the reins of power into our own hands. In the international situation [we have] the attempt to conclude a separate peace, which is the plan of the imperialistic bourgeoisie, and is directed against the proletariat. The internal situation is thus closely bound up with the external. We have arrived at a moment when the seizure of power will give us the means of leading the revolution and the country toward creative ends. Upon seizing the power we shall be forced to bring our slogans into life, [and] to realize our program immediately. We must organize everything. When in power we shall have to carry on wholesale terror. The general situation is such that an armed insurrection is inevitable, and our whole problem is to get ready for it. . . . We face a very essential problem—to have all mass propaganda focused on the conditions of the [present] moment. We must call together all agitators . . . and tell them how to conduct the agitation. Steps must be taken to conduct our agitation in accordance with a definite plan. The Executive Committee has worked out a number of theses which are herewith presented to the assembly. The external conditions of the country must first be characterized, then the internal. We must break up the illusions about the Constituent Assembly. We must tell the masses that the strength and power of the Constituent Assembly are the strength and power of one class or another. And if we want the Constituent Assembly to be ours, we must first take power into our hands. It may well happen that we shall not succeed in taking power; in that case the elemental wave of excitement will roll over our heads. To prevent this we must take the power into our hands. In our agitation we must emphasize that the collision is inevitable. We are facing the most critical hour of civil war—the armed struggle of two hostile classes. To save the revolution our policies must be not only defensive but also offensive. . . . We must calculate the moment when it is best for the offensive to begin. . . . These are the salient points. . . .

Nevsky: As a representative of the military organization I must call your attention to a number of difficulties confronting us. The [Bolshevik] Military Organization suddenly began to move to the Right. We must distinguish two questions: those of (1) fundamental principles, and (2) their practical realization. With reference to the resolution of the Central Committee the Military Organization pointed out that this resolution has left unconsidered a number of conditions, namely, that the poor peasants are also taking a part in the revolution. Instead of the village turning away from us it has only begun to come to us. We receive information from numerous places that the Bolsheviks are beginning to become popular. The decisive factor in the revolution is, of course, the working class. . . . But we must not on that account neglect the spirit of the peasant masses; if we do we shall not win the victory. In quite a number of gubernias [provinces] . . . the peasants say that in case of an insurrection they will not give us any bread. Absolutely nothing has been done to stir up the village. An armed uprising of the proletariat here in Petersburg is a feasible thing. The whole garrison will come out at the call of the Soviet. . . . But we cannot confine the insurrection to Petersburg. How will Moscow and the provinces react to this? Can the Central Committee give us the assurance that Russia as a whole will support us? We all realize that the moment is ripe. But are we ready? Have we the majority which will guarantee freedom? From the report it is quite clear that we are not ready, and the question stands thus: If we should come out, we shall find ourselves isolated from the rest of Russia. We have no data concerning the situation on the railroads. And are you sure that the 5th Army will not be sent against us? . . . Neither the Military Organization nor the Central Committee has this assurance. . . . The Military Organization will come out [for us] any time, but I cannot tell what this will accomplish. . . . The resolution of the Central Committee which raised the question [of insurrection] with such an urgency should have considered the other question of the preparedness of the masses. The Petrograd Committee must call the attention of the Central Committee to the necessity of preparing the provinces. . . .

Fenigstein moved that reports be made on conditions in the different districts. The motion was carried. . . .

Kharitonov: . . . The joint session of the Petrograd Committee, the Central Committee, the district committee, and the Moscow [people disclosed] that there is a general lack of enthusiasm. In Krasnoe Selo, where we have a large organization of some 50,000 members, only 500 may be expected to come here [Petrograd]; the rest will remain in Krasnoe Selo undecided. Krasnoe Selo is living through a mood of depression. Drunkenness is prevalent even among our comrades. From a military point of view the sailors are a very poor lot. A good many of them have been sent back from the front because they did not know how to handle arms. As for the post and telegraph employees, we have in our organization from

140 to 150 members. . . . The telegraph operators are mostly Kadets and have very little sympathy with us. At a decisive moment there may be sufficient force to occupy the telegraph and other important positions.

Slutskaya: Regarding the military situation in our district, I can say that military instruction is being given in the factories and industrial plants. There is not much desire to take part in the insurrection.

Latsis (Vyborg district): A serious concentration of interest in events is observable among the masses. In addition to the district committees a new central organization grew up from the bottom. . . . The masses will support us.

Kalinin (Lesnovsky sub-district): We have decided to investigate the conditions; as yet the business is badly managed. We have decided to get in contact with the army units. We receive telegrams from Finland and from the front protesting against the uprising of the Bolsheviks. On the other hand, over the head of the army organization, delegates are arriving from the front, and their demands clearly indicate a militant frame of mind. It proves that the army committees are not with us, and that they do not express the wishes of the masses. We have a Red Guard; only 84 rifles.

Naumov (Vyborg district): There is a marked dissatisfaction among the masses . . . and a feeling of suppressed indignation in connection with the evacuation [of Petrograd] and the [laying] off of the workmen.

Menzhinskaya: With regard to arms, conditions are very bad. In the committee there are only 6 rifles, in one factory 100, in another 20. It is difficult to estimate the spirit of the workers.

Pakhomov (second city district): The frame of mind is better than it was on July 3 to 5. The Red Guard is badly organized. We have 50 rifles, 3,000 cartridges. From 60 to 80 are receiving [military] instruction. . . .

Ravich (Moscow district): In the factories there is a turbulent state of feeling. The masses will rise only at the call of the Soviet, but very few will respond to the call of our party. The organs created during the Kornilov days are still intact. . . .

Hessen (Narva district): In general, there is no desire to rise. Where our influence is strong, the spirit is cheerful and eager. Among the backward masses there is an indifference to politics. But our party has not lost its authority. . . . We have several hundred rifles, but there is no concentration point and our military forces are scattered. . . .

Vinokurov (Neva district): The state of mind is in our favor. The masses are alert. We have no Red Guard. . . .

Comrade from the Obukhov factory: Previously the Obukhov factory stood for the defensists. But now there is a break in our favor. The attendance at our mass meetings is from five to seven thousand . . . we have 2,000 in the Red Guard, 500 rifles, 1 machine gun, and 1 armored car. . . . We have organized a revolutionary committee. The factory will no doubt respond to the call of the Petrograd Soviet.

Pervukhin (Okhtensky district): There is no desire among the workers to rise. In the factories the Black Hundreds [nationalistic anti-Semites] have raised their heads.

Prokhorov (Petersburg district): Where our influence is strong the attitude is one of watchfulness—otherwise the masses are apathetic. . . . Generally there is a complete disorganization in the district. Even if the Soviet should issue a call for an uprising, certain factories (ours for example) will not respond.

Axelrod (Rozhdestvensky district): The attitude is one of watchfulness. In case of an offensive on the part of the counter-revolution we shall offer resistance, but to a call to insurrection the workers will hardly respond. There is discouragement due to the [laying] off of workers in connection with the evacuation of factories. The influence of the anarchists is considerably on the increase. . . .

Rakhia (Finnish district): The Finns all feel that the sooner the better. . . .

[*A discussion of general principles followed.*]

Kalinin: The resolution of the Central Committee is the best it has ever passed. That resolution summons our organization to direct political action. We are confronted with an armed insurrection but our stumbling-block is the practical aspect of the situation. When that insurrection will take place, we cannot say—possibly in a year's time. . . .

Toward the end of the session Latsis announced that a new conspirative center[1] had just been organized in connection with the [Petrograd] Soviet whose membership is not exclusively Bolshevik. . . .

---

[1] [The Military-Revolutionary Committee—ED.]

Lenin's Plans

On or about October 17 Lenin sent for the leaders of the Bolshevik Military Organization to discuss preparations for the armed uprising. The meeting was described in the memoirs of several of the participants.

a) Podvoisky's Account

Lenin summoned V. I. Nevsky, Antonov-Ovseyenko, Rakovsky and Podvoisky to meet him in the underground, in order absolutely to make sure of the preparations for the uprising. Antonov-Ovseyenko declared that while he had no basis for judging the Petrograd garrison, he was sure that the fleet would come out at the first call, but it could hardly arrive at Petrograd in time. Nevsky and Podvoisky indicated that the mood of the troops of the garrison was clearly sympathetic to the uprising, but that nevertheless a certain delay of ten to fifteen days was necessary in order to present this question directly and decisively in each military unit, and to prepare technically for the uprising, the more so since the units that came out in the month of July . . . had been partly discharged and partly demoralized, and would come out only if they were sure of a move by other units, while the readiness for a move on the part of other units which had formerly been reactionary had to be tested. The point was also made by Podvoisky that Kerensky could rely on special combined units and other reactionary units from the front that were capable of obstructing the success of the uprising.

Comrade Nevsky indicated that as regards the sailors from Helsingfors and elsewhere there could be no doubt but that the movement of the fleet to Petrograd would meet with colossal difficulties, for the uprising would certainly evoke counteraction by the officers

* *Krasnaya Gvardiya v Oktiabrskie Dni* [The Red Guard in the October Days] (Moscow and Leningrad: State Press, 1927), pp. 16–17. (Editor's translation.)

and consequently their arrest, and then the sailors taking their place would have a hard time navigating the ships through the mine fields and doing battle at Petrograd.

In general, all agreed on the idea of postponing the insurrection a few weeks, believing it necessary to use this time for the most energetic preparations for the uprising in Petrograd, in the provinces, and at the front. . . .

However, none of these conclusions convinced or shook Vladimir Ilyich in any way. He said that all the decrees of the new power would in essence be only a confirmation of what was already being partially carried out, and consequently the first message from the new power would automatically confirm what the provinces and the front had long been waiting for, and finally that a delay in the uprising would permit the government and its parties, undoubtedly aware of the uprising and preparing to meet it, to use the period of postponement to prepare still more. "An uprising before the Congress [of Soviets]," said Lenin, "is especially important so that this Congress, whatever it is like, will face the accomplished fact of the seizure of power by the working class and will immediately confirm this."

b) *Antonov-Ovseyenko's Account**

. . . I was summoned to Comrade Lenin, who at that time had gone underground to hide. "Let's go. Ilyich wants to see you. Don't delay!" I hastily sent some visitors on their way, and gave the necessary directions to my deputy in the secretariat of the Military-Revolutionary Committee. Comrades Nevsky and Podvoisky hurried me out with them. In the pale twilight of the evening our automobile wound a long way through various crooked streets, finally stopping on one of the little streets of the Vyborg district. We went through a couple of alleys, watching carefully to see that no one was following us, and finally, fully convinced that we were leaving no

* "The Capture of the Winter Palace," *Proletarskaya Revoliutsiya* [Proletarian Revolution], no. 10 (1922), pp. 124–26. (Editor's translation.)

trail, we slipped one at a time through the doorway of one of the unsightly buildings. We gave the arranged knock and they immediately let us in. The tenant of the apartment, a stocky, elderly worker, easily recognized my companions. "Come in, Ilyich will be here right away." We waited a little. Well, who would have recognized our beloved comrade leader whom we thought we knew to the smallest wrinkle. In front of us stood a little old gray-haired man with glasses, hale and hearty and benevolent in appearance, looking like a cross between a teacher and a musician, perhaps a bookseller. Ilyich took off his wig and glasses, and sparkling with his usual humor, glanced around at us. "Well, what's new?" Our reports did not coincide. Podvoisky expressed doubt, Nevsky sometimes seconded him and sometimes took the assured tone of Ilyich; I talked about the situation in Finland. The sailors on the large ships were in an extremely revolutionary mood, part of the infantry also, but the crews of certain torpedo boats and submarines were less reliable. The Sveaborg artillerymen were still captives of the compromisers. The Kuban Cossacks posed a danger, but the Vyborg garrison would undertake not to let them out of Finland. Ilyich interrupted: "Can't you send the whole fleet to St. Pete?" No—in the first place the depth of the channel wouldn't permit it, then the large ships are leery of the submarines and torpedo boats, finally the sailors don't want to leave the front uncovered. "But shouldn't they understand that the Revolution is in greater danger in St. Pete than in the Baltic?" They don't understand it very well. "What can be done?" We can send two or three torpedo boats into the Neva and send a combined unit of sailors and Vyborg men, in all about three thousand. "Not much," says Ilyich, dissatisfied and reproachful. "And what about the Northern Front?" According to the reports of the representatives there the mood was fine and we could expect great help from them, but it was necessary to go there in order to find out exactly. "Go, you can't delay!"

Ilyich's conviction and firmness had the effect of firming me up and encouraging Comrade Nevsky, but Podvoisky persisted in his doubts. We carefully went out to the street. Right at the gateway we bumped into a tall figure, preparing to slip in on a bicycle. Could he be a spy? Just today the Provisional Government announced in the newspapers that it was on the trail of Lenin and Zinoviev and that the arrest of the Bolshevik leaders was inescapable. Comrade Nevsky went back into the building to warn them, and I, squeezing my revolver, walked around the corner. Podvoisky stopped at the next corner, and the bicycle started off. In two minutes Ilyich, again unrecognizable, had gone to another hide-out. We quickly stepped toward the automobile.

Formation of the Military-Revolutionary Committee

While the Bolshevik leadership debated the question of an uprising, the Petrograd Soviet under the presidency of Trotsky belatedly took steps to establish its command over the regiments of the Petrograd garrison. To this end, a "Military-Revolutionary Committee of the Soviet," first voted on October 12, was activated on October 20, ostensibly to protect the city from counter-revolution or surrender to the Germans. The committee was nominally chaired by a Left Socialist Revolutionary soldier named Lazimir, but dominated by the leaders of the Bolshevik Military Organization.

a) Trotsky's *History* *

Attempting to kindle the patriotism of the masses by threatening the loss of Petrograd, the Compromisers[1] introduced into the Soviet on October 9 a motion to create a "Committee of Revolutionary Defense," whose task should be to take part in the defense of the capital with the active cooperation of the workers. While refusing to assume responsibility for "the so-called strategy of the Provisional Government and in particular the removal of troops from Petrograd" the Soviet nevertheless had made no haste to express itself upon the substance of the order removing the soldiers, but had decided to test its motives and the facts upon which it was based. The Mensheviks had raised a protest: It is not permissible

---

* Leon Trotsky, *History of the Russian Revolution,* translated by Max Eastman (Ann Arbor: The University of Michigan Press, 1932, 1957), 3:91–94, 96–97, 99, 109–10, 112–13. Copyright © 1932 by The University of Michigan. Reprinted by permission.
    [1] [Mensheviks and SR's—ED.]

to interfere in the operative orders of the commanding staff. But it was only a month and a half since they had talked the same way about the conspiratorial orders of Kornilov, and they were reminded of this. In order to test the question whether the removal of the troops was dictated by military or political considerations, a competent body was needed. To the extreme surprise of the Compromisers the Bolsheviks accepted the idea of a "Committee of Defense." This committee should be the one to gather all data relating to the defense of the capital. That was an important step. Having snatched this dangerous weapon from the hands of the enemy, the Soviet remained in a position to turn the decision about removing the troops this way or that according to circumstances—but in any case against the government and the Compromisers.

The Bolsheviks quite naturally seized upon this Menshevik project of a military committee, for there had been conversations often enough in their own ranks about the necessity of creating in good season an authoritative Soviet committee to lead the coming insurrection. In the Military Organization of the party they had even drawn up plans for such a body. The one difficulty they had not yet got over was that of reconciling an instrument of insurrection with an elective and openly functioning Soviet, upon whose benches, moreover, sat representatives of the hostile parties. The patriotic proposal of the Mensheviks, therefore, came up most appropriately, and came up just in time to assist in the creation of a revolutionary headquarters—a body soon to be renamed "Military-Revolutionary Committee" and to become the chief lever of the revolution.

Two years after the events described above, the author of this book wrote in an article dedicated to the October revolution: "As soon as the order for the removal of the troops was communicated by Headquarters to the Executive Committee of the Petrograd Soviet . . . it became clear that this question in its further development would have decisive political significance." The idea of an insurrection began to take form from that moment. It was no longer necessary to invent a Soviet body. The real aim of the future committee was unequivocally brought out when in the same session Trotsky concluded his report on the withdrawal of the Bolsheviks from the Pre-Parliament with the exclamation: "Long live the direct and open struggle for a revolutionary power throughout the country!" That was a translation into the language of Soviet legality of the slogan: "Long live the armed insurrection!" . . .

In creating a commission to draw up regulations for the "Committee of Defense," the Executive Committee of the Petrograd

Soviet designated for the future military body such tasks as the following: to get in touch with the Northern front and . . . headquarters of the Petrograd district, with Centrobalt[2] and the regional soviet of Finland, in order to ascertain the military situation and take the necessary measures; to take a census of the personal composition of the garrison of Petrograd and its environs, also of the ammunition and military supplies; to take measures for the preservation of discipline in the soldier and worker masses. The formulae were all-inclusive and at the same time ambiguous: they almost all balanced on a fine line between defense of the capital and armed insurrection. However, these two tasks, heretofore mutually exclusive, were now in actual fact growing into one. Having seized the power, the Soviet would be compelled to undertake the military defense of Petrograd. The element of defense-camouflage was not therefore violently dragged in, but flowed to some extent from the conditions preceding the insurrection.

With this same purpose of camouflage a Social[ist] Revolutionary and not a Bolshevik was placed at the head of the commission on the "Committee of Defense." This was a young and modest intendant [military clerk], Lazimir, one of those Left Social[ist] Revolutionaries who were already traveling with the Bolsheviks before the insurrection—although, to be sure, not always foreseeing whither the course would lead. Lazimir's preliminary rough draft was edited by Trotsky in two directions: the practical plans relating to the conquest of the garrison were more sharply defined, the general revolutionary goal was still more glazed over. As ratified by the Executive Committee against the protest of two Mensheviks, the draft included in the staff of the Military-Revolutionary Committee the praesidiums of the Soviet and of the soldiers' section, representatives of the fleet, of the regional committee of Finland, of the railroad unions, of the factory committees, the trade unions, the party military organizations, the Red Guard, etc. The organizational basis was the same as in many other cases, but the personal composition of the committee was determined by its new tasks. It was assumed that the organizations would send representatives familiar with military affairs or standing near to the garrison. The character of an organ should be conditioned by its function.

Another new formation of this period was no less important. Under the direction of the Military-Revolutionary Committee there was created a Permanent Conference of the Garrison. The soldiers'

---

[2] [The Central Committee of the Baltic Fleet—Ed.]

section represented the garrison politically, the deputies being elected under the party symbols. The Garrison Conference, however, was to consist of the regimental committees which guided the daily lives of their units and thus constituted a more immediate practical "guild" representation. The analogy between the regimental and the factory committees is obvious. Through the mediation of the workers' section of the Soviet the Bolsheviks were able upon big political questions to rely confidently upon the workers. But in order to become masters in the factories it had been necessary to carry the factory and shop committees. The composition of the soldiers' section guaranteed to the Bolsheviks the political sympathy of the majority of the garrison. But in order to get the practical disposal of the military units it was necessary to rely directly on the regimental committees. This explains why in the period preceding the insurrection the Garrison Conference naturally crowded out the soldiers' section and moved to the center of the stage. The more prominent deputies in the section were also, by the way, members of the Conference. . . .

The regulations proposed by Lazimir were adopted by a majority of 283 votes against 1, with 23 abstaining. These figures, unexpected even to the Bolsheviks, gave a measure of the pressure of the revolutionary masses. The vote meant that the soldiers' section had openly and officially transferred the administration of the garrison from headquarters to the Military-Revolutionary Committee. The coming days would show that this was no mere gesture.

On that same day the Executive Committee of the Petrograd Soviet made public the creation under its supervision of a special department of the Red Guard. The matter of arming the workers, neglected under the Compromisers and even obstructed by them, had become one of the most important tasks of the Bolshevik Soviet. The suspicious attitude of the soldiers toward the Red Guard was already far in the past. On the contrary, almost all the resolutions of the regiments contained a demand for the arming of the workers. From now on the Red Guard and the garrison stand side by side. Soon they will be still more closely united by a common submission to the Military Revolutionary Committee. . . .

The [October 16] session of the Soviet took up the regulations of the Military-Revolutionary Committee. This institution had barely come into existence when it assumed in the eyes of the enemy an aspect growing every day more hateful. "The Bolsheviks make no answer," cried an orator of the opposition, "to the direct question: Are they preparing an attack? This is either cowardice or lack of confidence in their forces." The meeting greeted this remark with hearty laughter: the representative of the government party was demanding that the party of insurrection open the secrets of its heart to him. The new committee, continued the orator, is nothing else but "a revolutionary headquarters for the seizure of power." They, the Mensheviks, would not enter it. "How many are there of you?" cried a voice from the benches: there were indeed only a few Mensheviks in the Soviet, fifty altogether. But nevertheless it seemed authoritatively known to them that "the masses are not in favor of coming out." In his reply Trotsky did not deny that the Bolsheviks were preparing for a seizure of power: "We make no secret of that." But at present, he said, that is not the question. The government has demanded the removal of the revolutionary troops from Petrograd and to that "we have to answer yes or no." The regulations drafted by Lazimir were adopted by an overwhelming majority. The president [Trotsky] proposed to the Military-Revolutionary Committee to begin work on the following day. Thus one more forward step was taken. . . .

The decision to create a Military-Revolutionary Committee, first introduced on the 9th, was passed at a plenary session of the Soviet only a week later. The Soviet is not a party; its machinery is heavy. Four days more were required to form the Committee. Those ten days, however, did not go for nothing: the conquest of the garrison was in full swing, the Conference of Regimental Committees had demonstrated its viability, the arming of the workers was going forward. And thus the Military-Revolutionary Committee, although it went to work only on the 20th, five days before the insurrection, found ready to its hands a sufficiently well organized dominion. Being boycotted by the Compromisers, the staff of the Committee contained only Bolsheviks and Left Social[ist] Revolutionaries: that eased and simplified the task. Of the Social[ist] Revolutionaries only Lazimir did any work, and he was even placed at the head of the bureau in order to emphasize the fact that the Committee, whose president was Trotsky, and its chief workers Podvoisky, Antonov-Ovseyenko, Lashevich, Sadovsky, and Mekhonoshin, relied exclusively upon Bolsheviks. The Committee hardly met once in plenary session with delegates present from all the institutions listed in its regulations. The work was carried on through the bureau under the guidance of the president, with Sverdlov brought in upon all important matters. And that was the general staff of the insurrection.

The bulletin of the Committee thus modestly registers its first steps: commissars were appointed in the combatant units of the garrison and in certain institutions and store houses "for observation and leadership." This meant that, having won the garrison politically, the Soviet was now getting organizational control of it. The dominant role in selecting these commissars was played by the Military Organization of the Bolsheviks. Among its Petrograd members, approximately a thousand, there was no small number of resolute soldiers and young officers utterly devoted to the revolution, and who had since the July Days been tempered in the prisons of Kerensky. The commissars recruited from its midst found in the troops of the garrison a soil well prepared. The garrison considered them its own and submitted to their orders with complete willingness.

The initiative in getting possession of institutions came in most cases from below. The workers and clerical employees of the arsenal adjoining the Peter and Paul Fortress themselves raised the question of the necessity of establishing control over the giving out of arms. A commissar sent there succeeded in stopping a supplemental arming of the junkers [cadets], held back 10,000 rifles on their way to the Don region, and smaller assignments to a number of suspicious organizations and persons. This control was soon extended to other arsenals and even to private dealers in weapons. It was only necessary to appeal to the committee of the soldiers, workers or clerical employees of the given institution or store, and the resistance of the administration would be immediately broken. Weapons were given out henceforth only upon the order of the commissars. . . .

The Military-Revolutionary Committee appointed three commissars to the district headquarters—Sadovsky, Mekhonoshin and Lazimir. Orders of the commander were to become effective only when countersigned by one of these three. At a telephone call from Smolny the staff sent an automobile for the delegation—the customs of the dual power were still in effect—but contrary to expectations this extreme politeness of the staff did not imply a readiness to make concessions.

After listening to the declaration of Sadovsky, Polkovnikov[3] stated that he did not recognize any commissars and had no need of any guardianship. To a hint from the delegation that along that road headquarters might meet with resistance from the side of the troops, Polkovnikov dryly answered that the garrison was in his hands and its submission was assured. "His assurance was sincere," writes Mekhonoshin in his memoirs. "We felt no affectation in it." For

[3] [Commander of the Petrograd Military District—Ed.]

the return trip to Smolny the delegates did not receive an official automobile.

A special session of the Conference, to which Trotsky and Sverdlov were summoned, adopted a decision: To consider the break with headquarters an accomplished fact, and make it the starting point for a further offensive. The first condition of success: The districts must be kept in touch with all stages and episodes of the struggle. The enemy must not be allowed to catch the masses unaware. Through the district soviets and committees of the party the information was sent into all parts of the town. The regiments were immediately informed of what happened. The instructions were confirmed: Carry out only those orders which are countersigned by the commissars. It was also suggested that they send out only the most reliable soldiers for patrol duty.

But headquarters also decided to take measures. Spurred on evidently by his compromisist allies, Polkovnikov called together at one o'clock in the afternoon his own conferences of the garrison, with representatives of the Central Executive Committee present. Anticipating this move of the enemy, the Military-Revolutionary Committee called an emergency conference of the regimental committees at eleven o'clock, and here it was decided to formulate the break with headquarters. The appeal to the troops of Petrograd and the environs drawn up at this meeting speaks the language of a declaration of war. "Having broken with the organized garrison of the capital, headquarters is a direct instrument of the counter-revolutionary forces." The Military-Revolutionary Committee disclaims all responsibility for the activities of headquarters, and standing at the head of the garrison takes upon itself "the defense of revolutionary order against counter-revolutionary attempts."

That was a decisive step on the road to insurrection.

b) Bulletin of the Petrograd Military-Revolutionary Committee*

In connection with the alarming political situation and to take the appropriate measures in this regard for the defense of

* From G. N. Golikov *et al.*, eds., *Oktiabrskoe Vooruzhennoe Vosstanie v Petrograde* [The October Armed Uprising in Petrograd] (Moscow: USSR Academy of Sciences, 1957), p. 226. (Editor's translation.)

Petrograd against counter-revolutionary moves and pogroms, the Petrograd Soviet of Workers' and Soldiers' Deputies has mobilized all its forces.

Confirmed by a general meeting of the Soviet, the Military-Revolutionary Committee got organized as of the 20th of this October and proceeded with the most intensive activity, while maintaining contact with the Headquarters of the Petrograd Military District.

In the make-up of the Military-Revolutionary Committee, besides members of the Soviet and representatives of the garrison, representatives have been brought in from the Central Committee of the Baltic Fleet, the Finland regional committee, local government, the Factory and Mill Committees and the trade unions, the Soviet of Peasants' Deputies, party military organizations, and others.

Uninterrupted guard duty by the members of the Military-Revolutionary Committee and the closest liaison with the district soviets and military units of the garrison of Petrograd and its environs were decided upon.

In the Military-Revolutionary Committee there is one representative from each of the regimental committees to serve as liaison.

Every morning at the report desk reports are to be presented by the representatives of the district and troop committees on the mood and state of affairs in each locality.

October 20

The first session of the Military-Revolutionary Committee has taken place. A report was presented by the organizing bureau on a series of basic tasks subject to decision by the meetings, and on the establishment of liaison service with units around the city and in the suburbs.

Also at a session of the bureau today a series of measures was adopted to guard against possible excesses in connection with the scheduled Holy Procession of Cossacks, and also for the defense of Petrograd.

Agitators have been dispatched around the city. Liaison with the brigade committees has been organized. A report on the state of affairs at Headquarters was heard.

Commissars have been dispatched to the line units of the garrison, certain institutions and storehouses, for observation, guidance, and organization of the appropriate measures of defense.

The Petrograd Soviet of Workers' and Peasants' Deputies has issued an appeal to the Cossacks explaining the political situation and the efforts of the counter-revolution.

The Defiance of Governmental Authority

The Bolshevik Revolution began in effect on October 22 when the Military-Revolutionary Committee issued a proclamation to the garrison ordering it to heed only the authority of the Soviet.

The proclamation can be found in Golikov, p. 234. The following translation is from Robert V. Daniels, *Red October: The Bolshevik Revolution of 1917* (New York: Charles Scribner's Sons, 1967), p. 122. Copyright © 1967 by Robert V. Daniels; this and following selections reprinted by permission of Charles Scribner's Sons and Martin Secker & Warburg Ltd.

At its meeting on the 21st of October the revolutionary garrison of Petrograd rallied around the Military-Revolutionary Committee of the Petrograd Soviet of Workers' and Soldiers' Deputies as its leading organ.

In spite of this, on the night of October 21–22 the headquarters of the Petrograd Military District failed to recognize the Military-Revolutionary Committee and refused to conduct its work in cooperation with the representatives of the soldiers' section of the Soviet.

By this act the headquarters breaks with the revolutionary garrison and the Petrograd Soviet of Workers' and Soldiers' Deputies.

By breaking with the organized garrison of the capital, the headquarters is becoming a direct instrument of the counter-revolutionary forces.

The Military-Revolutionary Committee disclaims all responsibility for the actions of the headquarters of the Petrograd Military District.

Soldiers of Petrograd!

1. The protection of the revolutionary order from counter-revolutionary incursions rests on you, under the direction of the Military-Revolutionary Committee.

2. Any directives for the garrison that are not signed by the Military-Revolutionary Committee are invalid.

3. All directives for today—the Day of the Petrograd Soviet of Workers' and Soldiers' Deputies—remain in full force.

4. Every soldier in the garrison has the obligation of vigilance, restraint, and undeviating discipline.

5. The revolution is in danger. Long live the revolutionary garrison!

Part Five
 # THE OCTOBER UPRISING

On the eve of the opening of the Second Congress of
Soviets Petrograd was effectively divided between two governments,
yet the proto-government of the Bolshevik Soviet had no specific
plans to act apart from enlisting the garrison, the fleet, and the Red
Guards to defend the Congress while it voted to depose the Kerensky regime. In fact it was the government's initiative that precipi-
tated the denouement, when Kerensky ordered his troops to close
down the Bolshevik press on the morning of October 24. The Bolshevik Central Committee, believing the Counter-Revolution was
under way, set in motion its maximum defensive procedures, only
to discover that the city was falling into the hands of pro-Soviet
forces with hardly a shot being fired, while Kerensky's government
was mired in internecine quarrels. Lenin entered the picture belatedly, although there is reason to believe that the moves of the
Soviet forces took on a more deliberately offensive character after
his appearance at Soviet headquarters in the Smolny Institute
during the night of October 24–25.

By the morning of October 25 events had clearly worked to suit
Lenin's highest hopes for a violent but speedy seizure of power. The
Military-Revolutionary Committee proclaimed the overthrow of the
Provisional Government and closed down its consultative body, the
Council of the Republic or "Pre-Parliament." After some delay,
during which Kerensky made his escape, Soviet troops surrounded
the Cabinet in their last stronghold, the Winter Palace of the
Tsars. The "siege" has been over-glamorized: some desultory skirm-
ishing was followed by the surrender of the defenders and the arrest
of the Cabinet ministers. Meanwhile the Second Congress of Soviets
was meeting in the Smolny Institute to ratify the overthrow of the
Provisional Government and commence legislating the new social
order.

The Government Raid

The seizure of the Bolshevik printing plant by a detachment of officer cadets at 5:30 a.m. on October 24 sent tremors of alarm rippling through the Soviet camp. The Military-Revolutionary Committee issued an emergency order to all its forces to mobilize for the defense of the revolution.

The "Circular of the Petrograd Military-Revolutionary Committee" is from Golikov, p. 290. (Editor's translation.)

Soldiers! Workers! Citizens!

The enemies of the people have gone over to the offensive during the night. The Kornilovites at Headquarters are trying to pull cadets and shock battalions in from the outskirts. The Oranienbaum cadets and the shock troops at Tsarskoe Selo have refused to move. A traitorous blow is being devised against the Petrograd Soviet of Workers' and Soldiers' Deputies. The newspapers "Rabochi Put" [Worker's Path] and "Soldat" [Soldier] have been closed and the printing plant sealed up. The campaign of the counter-revolutionary plotters is directed *against the All-Russian Congress of Soviets* on the eve of its opening, *against the Constituent Assembly, against the people.* The Petrograd Soviet of Workers' and Soldiers' Deputies is standing up to defend the revolution. The Military-Revolutionary Committee is leading the resistance to the attack of the plotters. The whole garrison and the whole proletariat of Petrograd are ready to deal a crushing blow to the enemies of the people.

The Military-Revolutionary Committee decrees:

1. All regimental, company, and crew committees, together with the commissars of the Soviet, and all revolutionary organizations must meet in constant session, and concentrate in their hands all information about the plans and actions of the plotters.

2. Not a single soldier shall become separated from his unit without the permission of the committee.

3. Two representatives from each unit and five from each district soviet shall immediately be sent to the Smolny Institute.

4. Report all actions of the plotters immediately to the Smolny Institute.

5. All members of the Petrograd Soviet and all delegates to the

All-Russian Congress of Soviets are summoned immediately to the Smolny Institute for a special session.

The counter-revolution has raised its criminal head.

All the gains and hopes of the soldiers, workers, and peasants are threatened with great danger. But the forces of the revolution immeasurably surpass the forces of its enemies.

The people's cause is in firm hands. The plotters will be crushed.

No vacillation or doubts. Firmness, steadfastness, perseverance, decisiveness. Long live the revolution!

The Central Committee's Response

The Bolshevik Central Committee convened in the Smolny Institute shortly after the closing of the newspapers on October 24, to consider emergency steps. The minutes reveal little plan for revolutionary action apart from staving off the government's offensive.

They are contained in *Protokoly Tsentralnogo Komiteta RSDRP-B, Avgust 1917–Fevral 1918* [Minutes of the Central Committee of the RSDWP-B, August 1917–February 1918], 2nd edition (Moscow, 1958), pp. 119–121. (Editor's translation.)

Minutes of the Session of the Central Committee of the RSDWP(B).24 October [6 November]

Attending: Dzerzhinsky, Kamenev, Nogin, Lomov (Oppokov), Miliutin, Ioffe, Uritsky, Bubnov, Sverdlov, Trotsky, Vinter (Berzin)

Comrade Kamenev proposes that today no member of the Central Committee be allowed to leave Smolny without the special decision of the Central Committee. Adopted.

To arrange with the Executive Commission [of the Petrograd

Bolshevik Committee] regarding their duty watch both at Smolny and at the Petrograd Committee. Adopted.

AGENDA

1. Report of the Military-Revolutionary Committee.
2. The Congress of Soviets.
3. On the plenary meeting of the Central Committee.

1. Report of Comrade Kamenev.

Reports on the negotiations with the representatives of Headquarters.

2. On the printing plant and the newspaper.

Decided: To immediately send a guard detail to the printing plant and take care of the immediate issue of the regular number of the newspaper.

3. On the relation to the Bureau of the Central Executive Committee.

Comrade Nogin insists on the necessity of clarifying the relation to the Bureau of the Central Executive Committee, since the railroad workers are following the decisions of the Central Executive Committee, and in case of disagreement with the latter we will be cut off from the rest of Russia.

The other comrades protest against this fear concerning the railroad workers.

Comrade Trotsky proposes putting two members of the Central Committee at the disposal of the Military-Revolutionary Committee to organize liaison with the postal and telegraph and railroad workers; a third member of the Central Committee, for observation of the Provisional Government. In regard to the Central Executive Committee with whatever of its delegates are present at today's session, to declare that the Central Executive Committee, whose mandate has long ago expired, is undermining the cause of revolutionary democracy.

Comrade Vinter expresses the view that it is risky to scatter the Central Committee, therefore it is better to bring in not just members of the Central Committee.

Comrade Kamenev considers it necessary to make use of yesterday's negotiations with the Central Executive Committee, which now have been violated by the closing of *Rabochi Put*, therefore the break with the Central Executive Committee must be accomplished on just this basis. He further considers it necessary to enter into negotiations with the Left SR's and enter into political contact with them.

Comrade Sverdlov considers it necessary to assign Comrade Bubnov for liaison with the railroad workers and with the postal and telegraph employees. He proposes that our comrades in the Bureau of the Central Executive Committee quickly declare their non-solidarity with the latter.

The vote is taken on Comrade Trotsky's first proposal on delegating members of the Central Committee for specified functions: (1) the railroad workers; (2) the post office and telegraph; (3) the food supply. Adopted.

Comrade Bubnov—to the railroad workers.

Comrade Dzerzhinsky—the post office and telegraph.

Comrade Dzerzhinsky speaks and proposes Comrade Liubovich, who has contact with the post office and telegraph.

Comrade Dzerzhinsky is made responsible; he is to organize this matter.

Comrade Miliutin is assigned to organize food supply affairs.

Comrade Podvoisky is assigned to organize observation of the Provisional Government and the disposition of its forces.

(A view expressed against Comrade Podvoisky.)

It is assigned to Comrade Sverdlov.

It is proposed to assign three men for negotiations with the Left SR's; one is proposed.

Comrade Kamenev and Comrade Vinter are assigned.

Comrades Lomov and Nogin are assigned to inform Moscow immediately about everything that is happening here.

The Moscow people report that at least one man needs to go to Moscow.

Comrade Miliutin proposes to establish permanent contact with Moscow; therefore not to send Lomov and Nogin, but only one of them; tomorrow one will go, and in a few days the other.

Comrade Trotsky proposes setting up a reserve headquarters at the Peter-Paul Fortress and to this end assigning one member of the Central Committee there.

Comrade Kamenev considers that in case of the destruction of Smolny, it is necessary to have a support point on the "Aurora," but Uritsky introduces a correction regarding a torpedo boat.

Comrade Trotsky insists that the political point be at the Peter-Paul Fortress.

Comrade Sverdlov proposes assigning over-all observation to Comrade Lashevich, not to a member of the Central Committee.

It is decided to furnish all members of the Central Committee with passes to the Fortress.

General observation to be assigned to Lashevich and Blagonravov. Sverdlov is assigned to maintain constant liaison with the Fortress.

The Disintegration of the Provisional Government

While the Bolsheviks were rallying their forces against the government, Kerensky was vainly attempting to win an endorsement of his leadership from the Pre-Parliament. The response was a resolution that in effect implied a vote of no confidence.

The resolution was reported in the newspaper *Rech* ["Speech"], October 25, 1917, and translated in Browder & Kerensky, *The Russian Provisional Government*, pp. 1779–80.

Following Dan, L. Martov spoke on behalf of the Internationalists. He declared that the Internationalists will not stand in the same ranks with the Kornilovites, and that if a conflict becomes unavoidable as a result of the policy which has been pursued to date, they will not be able to suppress the uprising. (Applause from the left.) "The language of Kerensky, who spoke about the movement of the rabble when the question concerned the movement of a significant part of the proletariat and the army, cannot be called anything else but a language of challenge to civil war. Only a government that is guided by the interests of the democracy can deliver the country from the horrors of a civil war." (Applause from the left.)

. . . After the recess, A. V. Peshekhonov, presiding, stated that two [resolutions] . . . had been submitted. The first formula, submitted by the Mensheviks, the Internationalists, the Left Socialist Revolutionaries, and the Socialist Revolutionaries, read [as follows]: "The recently developing revolutionary movement with the aim of seizing power threatens to provoke a civil war and create favorable conditions for pogroms and for the mobilization of Black Hundred counter-revolutionary forces. It will have the inevitable result of frustrating the Constituent Assembly and of bringing about a new military catastrophe and the collapse of the revolution under conditions of economic paralysis and the complete disintegration of the country. The success of the aforesaid agitation is due not only to the objective conditions of war and disorder, but also to the delay in carrying out urgent measures, and therefore it is, above all, necessary to issue a decree on the transfer of land to the jurisdiction of land committees, and to take a vigorous stand in foreign policy, proposing that the Allies proclaim the conditions of peace and enter into peace negotiations. In order to combat manifestations of anarchy and [to prevent] an outbreak of pogroms, it is necessary to adopt immediate measures for their liquidation and to create for this purpose, in Petrograd, a Committee of Public Safety consisting of representatives of municipal governments and of organs of the revolutionary democracy, acting in contact with the Provisional Government."

The second formula was submitted by the cooperative organizations and the Party of the People's Freedom. This formula read: "Having heard the report of the Minister-President, the Provisional Council of the Russian Republic declared that, in the struggle against traitors to the native land and to the cause of the revolution who have resorted to the organization of an open revolt in the capital, in the face of the enemy and on the eve of the Constituent Assembly, the Provisional Council will give its full support to the Government and urges that the most decisive measures be adopted for suppressing the revolt. . . ."

The first resolution received 123 votes for and 102 against, with 26 abstentions. . . . The session closed at 8:30 P.M.

The Occupation of Key Points

Bolshevik commissars, sometimes with armed detachments and sometimes without, were assigned during the afternoon and evening of October 24 to assert the Soviet's authority over various public buildings and installations. S. S. Pestkovsky, a delegate to the Congress of Soviets, recounted his assignment to take over the telegraph office in his memoirs, "On the October Days in St. Pete," *Proletarskaya Revoliutsiya* [Proletarian Revolution], no. 10 (1922), pp. 95–97. (Translated in Daniels, *Red October*, pp. 141–3.)

Dzerzhinsky ran up to me with a paper in his hand: "You and Comrade Leshchinsky are instructed to take over the main telegraph. Here is the mandate of the MRC that appoints you commissar of the telegraph. Go right away!"

"How do I take over the telegraph?" I asked.

"The Kexholm Regiment is on guard there, and they are on our side," answered Dzerzhinsky.

I didn't question any more. The assignment at first didn't seem very hard to me, since I was the director of our Petrograd postal-telegraph cell and knew almost all our Bolsheviks there. I found Comrade Leshchinsky, and we set off together. Neither of us had a revolver. When we were getting in the car we both had the same strange, tormenting tension in our minds: here it is, the decisive move of the proletariat that we have been waiting for for decades. How will it end?

Could it still be defeated?

The bitter experience of the July Days did not give us complete confidence in victory.

We decided to work this way. The Provisional Government's commander of the telegraph was a personal acquaintance of Leshchinsky—Staff-Captain Longva, at the time a Menshevik-Internationalist, now a Communist. We would have to talk with him and make sure of his cooperation. Then we would talk with our cell and at once proceed with the "seizure."

It turned out somewhat differently. Comrade Longva, "having no directive from his organization," refused to cooperate with us and only promised "not to interfere." And at the conference with the cell we realized that in the whole telegraph office, among three thousand employees, there was not a single Bolshevik, and only one Left SR, Khaurov; he reported to us that the whole mass of employees was very hostilely inclined against the Bolsheviks. [Unknown to Pestkovsky, all the Bolshevik members of the union were Post Office employees.]

The situation was extremely difficult. But at this point Comrade Liubovich arrived from Smolny to help us. The three of us felt stronger and went to talk with the guards.

When the guards, headed by some lieutenant, saw our mandate from the MRC, they promised to cooperate with us. Then, on October 24 about five o'clock, we three, accompanied by the commander of the guard, went into the main hall of the telegraph and up to the President of the union of postal and telegraph workers, Mr. King (a Right SR), and declared that we were taking over the telegraph. King declared that he was going to throw us out. Then Comrade Liubovich called two Kexholm men and stationed them at the switchboard.

The women working in the office began to scream and cry. The representatives of the "committee" deliberated and arrived at a compromise. They would agree that "the commissar could sit in the room" on condition that we withdraw the soldiers from the room.

We agreed. I "held forth" in the telegraph office, Liubovich went out to "strengthen" the guard, and Leshchinsky went off to the room of the union, in a neighboring building, as a "reserve."

At 8 P. M. of the same day a guard of cadets, specially ordered by the Petrograd Military District, arrived to "replace" the Kexholm men. The Kexholm guard, "cultivated" by Liubovich, declared they wanted to go on guarding the telegraph.

The cadets left.

Lenin Responds to the Action

Lenin was still in hiding on October 24. Hearing reports of the government's moves and the Soviet's counter-moves, he penned a note demanding implementation of his plan for insurrection before the Congress of Soviets. The document was long cited as proof of Lenin's leadership of the uprising, but recent Soviet scholarship, doubting that it was ever delivered, has recognized it as evidence of Lenin's lack of control of events. The "Letter to the Members of the Central Committee," is translated in V. I. Lenin, *Selected Works* (Moscow: Foreign Languages Publishing House, 1951), vol. 2, part 1, 196–8.

Comrades,

I am writing these lines on the evening of the 24th. The situation is critical in the extreme. It is absolutely clear that now, in truth, to delay the uprising would be fatal.

I exhort [my] comrades with all my strength to realize that everything now hangs on a thread; that we are confronted by problems which are not solved by conferences or congresses (even congresses of Soviets), but exclusively by peoples, by the masses, by the struggle of the armed masses.

The bourgeois onslaught of the Kornilovites and the removal of Verkhovsky[1] show that we must not wait. We must at all costs, this very evening, this very night, arrest the government, first having disarmed the cadets (defeated them, if they resist), and so forth.

We must not wait!! We may lose everything!!

The value of the seizure of power immediately will be the defence of the people (not of the congress, but of the people, the army and the peasants in the first place) from the Kornilovite government, which has driven out Verkhovsky and has hatched a second Kornilov plot.

Who must take power?

That is not important at present. Let the Military-Revolutionary Committee take it, or "another institution" which will declare that it will relinquish the power only to the true representatives of the interests of the people, the interests of the army (the immediate proposal of peace), the interests of the peasants (the land to be taken immediately and private property abolished), the interests of the starving.

All districts, all regiments, all forces must mobilize themselves at once and immediately send their delegations to the Military-Revolutionary Committee and to the Central Committee of the Bolsheviks with the insistent demand that under no circumstances should the power be left in the hands of Kerensky and Co. until the 25th—not under any circumstances; the matter must be decided without fail this very evening, or this very night.

History will not forgive revolutionaries for procrastinating when they could be victorious today (and will certainly be victorious today), while they risk losing much tomorrow, in fact, risk losing everything.

If we seize power today, we seize it not in opposition to the Soviets but on their behalf.

The seizure of power is the business of the uprising, its political purpose will become clear after the seizure.

It would be a disaster, or a sheer formality, to await the wavering vote of October 25. The people have the right and are in duty bound to decide such questions not by a vote, but by force; in critical moments of revolution, the people have the right and are

[1] [Minister of War, thought sympathetic to the Left—ED.]

in duty bound to direct their representatives, even their best representatives, and not to wait for them.

This is proved by the history of all revolutions; and it would be an infinite crime on the part of the revolutionaries were they to let the moment slip, knowing that upon them depends the *salvation of the revolution,* the proposal of peace, the salvation of Petrograd, salvation from famine, the transfer of the land to the peasants.

The government is tottering. It must be *given the death-blow* at all costs.

To delay action will be fatal.

Trotsky on Power through the Soviets

Addressing the Petrograd Soviet on the evening of October 24, Trotsky was still able to deny that a deliberate insurrection was intended prior to the Congress of Soviets. After the Bolsheviks' victory he suggested that these remarks were a dissimulation, but there is more reason to believe that Trotsky was trying to correct the record after the fact.

Trotsky's speech was reported in the Bolshevik paper *Rabochi Put* (The Worker's Path), October 26, 1917, and reprinted in his *Sochineniya* (Works), vol. 3, part 1, pp. 51–53; editor's translation. This version may be compared with the briefer report in *Izvestia,* October 25, 1917, translated in Golder, *Documents of Russian History, 1914–1917,* pp. 616–617.

After recounting the history of the conflict with the headquarters of the Military District, Comrade Trotsky reports on the whole series of attempts on the part of the Provisional Government to pull troops into Petrograd against the revolution. But all such attempts have been paralyzed by the Military-Revolutionary Committee.

We are not afraid to take on responsibility for the preservation of revolutionary order in the city. Today the Military-Revolutionary Committee declares to the population of Petrograd that "The Petrograd Soviet of Workers' and Soldiers' Deputies takes on the maintenance of the revolutionary order from counter-revolutionary and pogromist depredations."

Today a delegation from the city administration visited us. The delegation asked us: how do we regard the maintenance of order in the city? The government has no forces, no power—they see this. The delegation even repeated the rumor that the government is proposing to turn the power over to the city administration.

We answered the delegates from the city administration that in the interest of upholding revolutionary order we were ready to coordinate our activity with the activity of the City Duma. A representative of the Executive Committee of the Petrograd Soviet has been assigned to the city government ever since the Kornilov days. Corresponding to that, a representative of the city administration will join the Military-Revolutionary Committee of the Petrograd Soviet.

The delegation furthermore asks us about the uprising and the move. On this question we told them that it had more than once been discussed by us here. We answered the delegation:

"All Power to the Soviets"—This is our slogan. In the impending period of time—the period of the session of the All-Russian Congress of Soviets—this slogan must be implemented. Whether this leads to an uprising or a move depends not only and not so much on the Soviets as on those who hold state power in their hands contrary to the unanimous will of the people.

The Military-Revolutionary Committee arose not as an organ of insurrection but on the base of the self-defense of the revolution. When the government of Kerensky decided to disarm Petrograd and remove its troops from here, we said that in the interest of defending the revolution we could not allow this. When yesterday [actually, early that morning] this government closed two newspapers enjoying an enormous influence on the Petrograd proletariat and garrison, we said that we could not suffer the stifling of free speech, and decided to restore publication of the papers. We assigned the honored duty of guarding the printing-plant of the revolutionary papers to the valiant soldiers of the Litovsky Regiment and the Sixth Reserve Sapper Battalion.

Is this insurrection?

We have a quasi-power, which the people do not believe in and which does not believe in itself, for it is internally dead. This quasi-power is waiting for the sweep of the broom of history to clear a place for a genuine power of the revolutionary people.

The government has begun to mobilize the cadets, and at the same time they have given the cruiser *Aurora* orders to move off. Why, while calling in the cadets, has the government removed the sailors? The reasons are understandable. It has to do with those sailors before whom Skobelev[1] appeared with his hat in his hand in the Kornilov days to beg them to guard the Winter Palace against the Kornilovists. At that time the sailors of the *Aurora* complied with Skobelev's request. And now the government is trying to remove them. But our comrades the sailors asked advice from the Military-Revolutionary Committee. And today the *Aurora* is lying where it lay last night.

Tomorrow the Congress of Soviets opens. The task of the garrison and the proletariat is to place at the disposal of the Congress the concentrated force against which a governmental provocation would be shattered; and to deliver this force to the Congress undivided and undamaged.

When the Congress says that it is organizing the power, it will thereby complete the work that has been under way throughout the country. This will signify that the people, having liberated themselves from the power of the counter-revolutionary government, are convening their own Congress and creating their own power.

If the sham power makes a long-shot attempt to revive its own corpse, then the mass of the people, organized and armed, will give it a decisive rebuff, and the stronger the offensive of Reaction, the stronger this rebuff will be. If the government attempts to use the 24 or 48 hours that remain at its disposal to stick a knife in the back of the revolution, then we declare that the advance guard of the revolution will reply blow for blow, steel for iron.[2]

Lenin's Return to Smolny

Though ordered by the Central Committee not to leave his hideout for fear of arrest, Lenin decided late in the evening of October 24th to make his way to the Smolny Institute to take a hand in the events. His bodyguard Eino Rakhia described their trek in his memoirs, "The Last Underground of Vladimer Ilyich," *Krasnaya Letopis* [Red Chronicle], no. 1, 1934, pp. 88–9. (Translated in Daniels, *Red October*, pp. 158–61.)

[1] [The Menshevik Minister of Labor—ED.]
[2] [Original newspaper account here notes "Stormy, prolonged applause"—ED.]

I reported to V. I. He answered me, "Aha, this means it's beginning. The revolution is beginning. We must get to Smolny right away." I began to protest that this was impossible, that shooting had already begun on the streets in some places, and that when I came the streetcars had already stopped running. He didn't want to listen to me. I just had to agree with him.

I disguised him more or less: I found some impossibly old cap and the very worst clothes, that gave him a very contemptible appearance, and we set off hoping that in this get-up no one would really recognize him on the streets. I only warned him not to talk with anyone, so that he would not give himself away by his voice. We jumped on a streetcar that came along, and found it completely empty. The conductor was a woman. Suddenly V. I. asked her, "Where are you going?" She said, "To the carbarn." I was scared. He had a characteristic voice, and he had often spoken at meetings; I thought she recognized him. But he continued, "Why are you going there?" She looked at him: "Why do you wonder? Don't you know what's happening? What kind of a worker are you that you don't know there's going to be a revolution? We're going to beat the bourgies." [1] I thought that if he talked any more she would recognize him. Lenin talked with her the whole way, and she never knew to this day that it was V. I.

At the corner of Botkinskaya and Nizhegorodskaya the streetcar turned toward the carbarns, and we continued on foot.

As we approached the Liteiny Bridge, I saw soldiers and Red Guards standing on it. I told V. I. that it was dangerous to cross. He said, "Where there are soldiers and Red Guards together, there is no danger." He stood in the crowd and then suddenly went on, in spite of the fact that they were not allowing anyone across the bridge. I decided not to leave him alone, and went after him.

We crossed the bridge and walked along Shpalernaya Street towards Smolny.

Up ahead two cadets of the artillery school, mounted on horses, approached. I noticed that they were talking about something, and I whispered to V. I. to go past them without attracting attention, while I stayed back. We had two falsified passes; we had erased and changed them very unskillfully. I gave him one and kept the other for myself. The cadets approached and asked for our passes. I made it appear that I did not understand, and raised my voice, and at this moment V. I. walked ahead. I had two revolvers in my pockets and I decided to open fire with them if they went after V. I. One

---

[1] [Russian *burzhui*, contemptuous slang for "bourgeois"—Ed.]

of them said to the other, "Well, what are you talking with that drunk for? Chuck it!" They spurred their horses and rode off.

When we got to Smolny, they would not let us through. It seems that they had changed the credentials of the delegates to the Congress—they had been white, but now they were red. A small crowd gathered around us. We stood there. "Well," I thought, "we've gotten here, and they ought to be able to recognize Vladimir Ilyich." But he was surprisingly calm. Suddenly I thought of a way out of the situation: I decided to carry the offensive to the guards. I began to shout, "What a mess, I'm a delegate and they won't let me through," and so on. I started a racket; the crowd supported me and pushed the two Red Guards aside, and we moved in. V. I. came last, laughing, satisfied with the favorable outcome. We went upstairs. V. I. stopped to sit down by a window, and sent me to get Stalin. Then Trotsky came, and someone else—I don't remember who. We went into a little room. V. I. sat at the end of the table.

At this point, Lieber, Dan and Gotz [two Mensheviks and an SR, attending the meeting of the All-Russian Central Executive Committee] came in from the hall. Dan took a bundle out of his overcoat pocket, and addressing Lieber and Gotz by their first names, offered them something to eat. As he was taking out a French roll with sausage and cheese, he cast a casual glance to the side and only then recognized Vladimir Ilyich. This stunned him so that he scraped his bundle up in his arms, and all three sprang out of the room. V. I. and the rest of us roared with laughter.

The Midnight Take-over

Simultaneously with or shortly after Lenin's arrival at the Smolny Institute around midnight on the 24th, and perhaps on his inspiration (though this is not documented), armed Bolshevik detachments were directed to seize the key points still under government control. Within the space of a few hours almost all important government buildings, utilities, and railroad stations were put under the guard of pro-Soviet forces, with practically no resistance and scarcely a shot.

a) M. M. Lashevich, the commissar assigned to the most important of these operations, briefly recounted his experience in "The October Uprising in Petrograd," published in the collection *Leningradskie Rabochie v Borbe za Vlast Sovetov* [The Leningrad Workers in the Struggle for Soviet Power] (Leningrad: State Press, 1924), p. 109. (Editor's translation.)

The Military-Revolutionary Committee decided to act. I was ordered to seize the new state bank, the treasury, the telephone exchange, the telegraph office, and the post office during the night.

On approaching the telephone exchange we captured a patrol of cadets. Forcing our way, we burst into the courtyard of the building, after capturing the armored car at the gate. Cadets started to come running into the courtyard. There was a moment when a clash seemed inevitable, and then it would have been woe to the cadets, for in that box (the courtyard of the telephone exchange) anyone who resisted would have been thrashed. By a stratagem we succeeded in avoiding bloodshed.

Hearing the rattle of rifle bolts, I loudly commanded, "Empty your cartridges." Evidently not realizing who was giving the command, the cadets began to unload their rifles, and the Kexholm Regiment men took advantage of this to push the cadets into groups and surround them. The telephone exchange was taken without a shot.

We succeeded in capturing the state bank and the treasury even more easily. The soldiers of the Semenovsky Regiment who were on guard declared that they too were for the Military-Revolutionary Committee, and would not relinquish their posts, considering this an insulting lack of confidence by the representative of the Military-Revolutionary Committee. To avoid delay we had to agree with this, though to assure their loyalty I nevertheless left some of the sailors and Kexholm men there. At the same time the treasury was occupied by a unit sent there, and we got word of the occupation of the post office and the telegraph office. By eight o'clock [on the morning of the 25th] all the orders of the Military-Revolutionary Committee had been executed.

b) The officer in charge of the troops employed by Commisar Lashevich, Alexei Zakharov, recalled how his company was abruptly alerted for the mission. His account, "From the October Days: How the Telephone Exchange was Captured in Petrograd in October 1917," appeared in *Krasnaya Letopis* [Red Chronicle], nos. 5–6, 1931, pp. 72–74. The translation given here is the editor's.

Zakharov, writing in 1931, avoided mentioning Lashevich by name, evidently because the latter, after rising to become deputy war commisar, had been expelled from the Communist Party shortly before his death in 1928. It will be noted how Zakharov claimed the leading role that Lashevich, writing seven years before, had attributed to himself.

On the 23rd of October, old style, 1917, an order was given the Petrograd garrison that the commanding staff should not absent themselves from the premises of the barracks. Therefore on the 24th of October, old style, since I was the Commander of the Fifth Company of the Kexholm Reserve Life-Guard Regiment, I spent the whole day with the regiment. (The regiment was in the barracks of the Horse Guard regiment situated on Konnogvardeisky Boulevard—now the Boulevard of the Trade Unions.)

Late in the evening, when I was already asleep in my clothes on a divan in the officers' meeting room, I was waked up by Lieutenant Smirnov of our regiment, a member of the regimental committee, and told that by order of the regimental committee, I must immediately go out with my company and assume the guard at the Petrograd city telephone exchange, and that as a member of the regimental and brigade committees I must do this without special orders from the regimental staff. I quickly went to my company and found the men already lined up with their weapons. The chairman of the regimental committee, Sergeant Smirnov of the machine-gun unit, informed me that I was being given responsibility to take the telephone exchange, which was being guarded by cadets of the Vladimirsky military school, and he added that I must do this as quickly as possible and if possible without fighting. Two commissars were assigned to work with me.[1] Of course, I understood that my move was the beginning of a "coup d'état" (the definition I thought of at that moment), but I decided not to refuse the assignment but to carry it out as best I could, especially since the mood of the soldiers was very reliable—I felt this at once with my first glance at them.

The Fifth Company, at whose head I marched with two of my companions (there was not one other officer in the company, not even for the platoons), moved first along the embankment, and then along Morskaya Street. At the corner of Morskaya (now Herzen Street) and Voznesensky (now Prospekt Maiorova) a detail of cadets tried to stop me, but of course a detail of three cadets could not even try to stop a company of full combat complement. With the units in closed ranks, I led the soldiers at a run to cover the distance from the corner to the gate [of the telephone building] and quickly ran with the company through the gateway, at the end of which the guard of the building had stationed an armored car, almost completely blocking passage from the gateway into the courtyard of the building, so that my soldiers had to run one at a time on both sides of the armored car, between it and the walls, to get through to the courtyard of the building.

My commissars and I were the first to enter the courtyard, and succeeded in barring the way to the armored car from the cadets who were already running from the guard quarters into the courtyard of the building. I commanded the cadets, "Port arms. Empty cartridges." And the intimidated cadets, without the officer commanding the guard among them, executed my command, which in my excitement I had given very harshly and authoritatively, while the commissars with me explained to the cadets the uselessness of resistance and promised them no harm. After this, we put the cadets under guard by the company, and we three went into the office of the telephone exchange, where my companions [Lashevich and Kaliagin] explained to the head of the exchange that revolutionary soldiers had seized it and that I was appointed commandant, and they proposed to remove the former commandant immediately from the building. After this the commissars left, saying that they were going to the Revolutionary Headquarters in Smolny.

Not being familiar with the premises of the telephone exchange, I found it difficult to post the guard. Then all the top authorities of the exchange—for some reason present in the building despite the unseasonable hour (it was late at night)—began to assert to me the complete madness of my actions. It was very hard for me to argue anything with them, and so I fell silent, and when the city chief himself—the Right SR G. I. Shreider—called me to the telephone and told me that I must either immediately clear out of the building or suffer the consequences of trial as a state criminal, I couldn't find anything better to say to him at that moment than to expostulate that I was executing an order of my immediate superior. . . .

The Seizure of Power

At mid-morning on October 25 the Military-Revolutionary Committee proclaimed the revolution victorious. The proclamation, "To the Citizens of Russia," is from Golikov, p. 351. (Editor's translation.)

The Provisional Government has been overthrown. State power has passed into the hands of the organ of the Petrograd Soviet of Workers' and Soldiers' Deputies—the Military-Revolutionary Committee, which stands at the head of the Petrograd proletariat and garrison.

The cause for which the people have been struggling—the immediate proposal of a democratic peace, the abolition of landlord property in land, workers' control over production, the creation of a Soviet government—this cause is assured.

Long live the revolution of the workers, soldiers, and peasants!

The Siege of the Winter Palace: The Attackers

By the afternoon of October 25th Bolshevik-led forces had surrounded the Winter Palace, where the Provisional Government was making its last stand. G. I. Blagonravov, the Bolshevik commissar of the Peter-Paul Fortress on the opposite side of the Neva River, recounted the somewhat impromptu preparations for attack in "The October Days in the Peter-Paul Fortress," *Proletarskaya Revoliutsiya* [Proletarian Revolution], no. 4 (1922), pp. 33–40. (Editor's translation.)

. . . About twelve o'clock I set off for Smolny in the former commandant's car with the firm intention of proposing to the Military Revolutionary Committee a plan of offensive action— to attack the Winter Palace, in which the Provisional Government was sitting under the protection of the cadets and shock troops.

The first person who caught my eye as I reached the second floor was Comrade Antonov-Ovseyenko. He pulled me into the quarters of the Military Revolutionary Committee, where Comrades Podvoisky and Chudnovsky were talking animatedly next to a map of Petrograd covered with flags.

My proposal for an attack on the Winter Palace was nothing new, since my comrades had themselves invited me in for this to begin with. Quickly we began to work out a plan of military action, and made an approximate count of our forces. The chief support point and base would be the Peter-Paul Fortress, which would be in touch with neighboring units and the *Aurora*. (Antonov went to the *Aurora*.) Military units would be on the side of Millionaya Street, the Nevsky Prospekt, and the other streets leading to the Winter Palace to isolate the Winter Palace with a solid ring and then at the first signal to gradually tighten this ring around the Palace. Barriers of nearby Bolshevik military units and factories were to be set up against the possible movement of unreliable Cossack units and cadet schools. These barriers would paralyze a possible blow at the rear of our troops attacking the Winter Palace.

It was necessary to carry this plan out immediately. The general offensive and bombardment of the Winter Palace would begin the same day, not later than nine o'clock in the evening, after everything was ready, on a special signal from the fortress. Antonov and I would work out the details of the plan on the spot at the fortress. We divided the units and the command between us and hurried over there, since every minute was valuable, and alarming news came in more and more often about the approach to Petrograd of Cossack units loyal to Kerensky.

Antonov went at once to the *Aurora*, moored at the Nikolaevsky Bridge, and Chudnovsky and I went in one automobile to the fortress. At the entrance of the Trinity Bridge I said good-by to Chudnovsky; he was headed for the Pavlov regiment, which he was to lead in its offensive against the Winter Palace. Chudnovsky promised to set up a road block on the Champs de Mars [Parade Ground] at the end of the Trinity Bridge, and I, for my part, would send out periodic patrols for liaison with this road block and set up machine-guns for long-range enfilade of the bridge (to prevent a possible attempt at raising it). . . .

We began to prepare for battle. The fortress could only fire machine-guns and rifles: the guns standing formidably on the parapets were not fit to be fired and were emplaced solely for better appearances (only one cannon fired, a muzzle-loader, to signal the hour). It was necessary to think about getting guns and setting them up. After a short search in the courtyard of the arsenal we found several three-inch guns which in external appearance seemed to us, non-artillerymen, in good order and suitable for use. By our combined efforts, under the direction of Kondakov, the guns were dragged out beyond the wall of the fortress to the "campground" (the campground was a small area between the fortress wall and the diversionary canal from the Neva, formerly the actual place for encampment of units of the garrison, but now simply an empty place). It did not appear to be possible to choose another position for the guns since without any equipment it was impossible to pull the guns up onto the fortress wall (we could not place the guns behind the walls, by reason of the nearness of the target—the Winter Palace, which it was possible to shell only by direct fire). With the onset of darkness Kondakov and Pavlov had to move the guns out from behind the piles of rubbish where we had put them for the time being, fearing that they would be noticed by an observer in the Palace, and place them in previously selected places right at the bank of the Neva. A small quantity of shells for the guns was found in the arsenal, and we requisitioned a further supply as a supplement from the munitions depot on the Vyborg Side, which was promptly sent.

Things were not so good with the artillerymen. The fortress company, as I have already pointed out, could not be considered reliable. For the past few days the officers in command of the company and a portion of the soldiers—residents of Petrograd—had not appeared for duty. But there was no choice. With pangs of anxiety we instructed Comrade Pavlov to designate several of the most reliable artillerymen and commanders to service the guns, and to send them out without delay to look over the guns and the places we had chosen. Soon there appeared before me a delegate from the fortress company and its commander (I don't remember his name), a young second lieutenant. They declared to me that they were empowered by the general assembly of the company to bring to our attention the fact that the company intended to remain neutral just as in the days July 3 to 5, and therefore they refused to detach artillerymen for the guns or in general to move out with weapons in hand no matter on whose side.

The situation had become critical. There were no other artillerymen. We quickly headed for the barracks of the fortress company. They were all turned out there; evidently they were waiting for the answer from their delegates. I explained to the gathering that the position they had taken would not withstand any criticism. I demanded in the name of the Petrograd Soviet that they submit to my commands, and I warned them that non-execution of them would bring extremely undesirable consequences. My declaration produced a great impression. The orders I affirmed to dispatch the required number of artillerymen to check the guns and execute the shelling of the Winter Palace with them were, after some hesitation, carried out, and a group of artillerymen headed by the commander of the company set off for the guns on the "campground."

At this point I received word of the arrival of Comrade Antonov with some sailors from the *Aurora*. Antonov reported his intention to bring the *Aurora* still closer to the Nikolaevsky Bridge, and perhaps even move it beyond the bridge up to the fortress itself. For liaison of the fortress with the *Aurora* a steam cutter was to be sent to Peter-Paul. I quickly took in the details of the further plan of action. We decided that after we had established the battle readiness of all the units surrounding the Winter Palace, and had moved the guns to the places prepared for them, a red signal would be hoisted on the flagpole in the fortress (a lantern indicating our readiness). Then the *Aurora* would open fire with its guns, at first in the air; in case of the non-surrender of the Provisional Government, the fortress would begin to fire live ammunition. And then, if the Winter Palace continued to resist after this, the *Aurora* would open real fire with its guns. We composed an ultimatum to the Provisional Government to surrender, giving it twenty minutes to consider this from the moment of receipt of the ultimatum.

The ultimatum was signed by Antonov and me. A scout from the bicyclists undertook to transmit it. We set the time of dispatch at half an hour before the signal of complete battle readiness of the fortress and the units surrounding the Winter Palace. Finally Antonov left. The cutter for liaison with the *Aurora* arrived simultaneously. It grew dark. A small unforeseen circumstance disrupted our plan: there was no lantern for the signal. After a long search we found one, but displaying it on the flagpole so that it could easily be seen presented great difficulties, and Tregubovich, who was involved in this matter, became terribly unnerved by the repeated failures.

At that point I headed for the guns. The October night had really set in. The lanterns flickered with a dim light, and their rays glimmered on the dark swells of the Neva. The life of the city went its usual way: the streetcars with their sharp bells and racket stretched in a row across the Trinity Bridge, and automobiles and the figures of pedestrians shone there. Nothing hinted at the October battle.

The band of artillerymen were huddled against the trunks of some huge willow trees, stripped of their leaves by the autumn cold. At a few paces the guns darkened into a motionless mass. It seemed to me that as we drew near the conversation was suddenly stilled, and the artillerymen acted as though they were not quite themselves. We approached more closely. The second lieutenant came to meet us and reported that they could not fire the guns since they were out of order—they had rusted through, and there was not a drop of oil in the recoil mechanisms, and at the first shot they could blow up. I suspected malice. A wave of terrible pain struck me in the head and my hand involuntarily reached for my revolver, but I caught myself in time. I questioned them. The non-com and the artillerymen asserted the same thing with one voice. I understood nothing about guns and therefore was helpless to catch them in a lie. I remembered that Pavlov had something to do with guns. I decided to asssign him to carry out an investigation once more, and in the event that the report of the unserviceability of the guns was not confirmed, to deal severely with the transgressors. These considerations I expressed directly to the artillerymen. The latter heard me out calmly, as it seemed, and even gladly received my statement about the appointment of Pavlov to carry out the investigation of the guns. The second lieutenant said to me in parting, "Of course you don't believe me, but I give you my word that I am speaking the absolute truth—it is extremely dangerous to fire the guns."

Meanwhile, in the direction of the Winter Palace we began to hear rifle fire, at first occasional, and then more and more frequent. Through our liaison I was informed that the shooting was being done by the Pavlov Regiment with the cadets planted in the palace. They phoned me several times from Smolny and pointed out the necessity of beginning right away.

I became agitated. In spite of the fact that everything was not ready, I sent our comrade off with the ultimatum for the palace.

Suddenly the door of the duty officer's room was thrown wide open and Antonov flew in through it, terribly alarmed. He threw himself at me with reproaches for the fact that I had not begun for so long. I briefly explained the situation that had developed and proposed that we go out to the guns, where Pavlov was already taking charge.

The darkness in the courtyard had become even thicker. The rain that fell not long before had made huge puddles, through which we splashed in the most merciless way. In the direction of the palace we heard vigorous rifle fire, and now and then a machine-gun stuttered. Our men were also shooting aimlessly from the fortress walls in the direction of the Embankment and the Winter Garden, from which now and then rifle fire by the cadets burst out in return.

Antonov, who had rather weak vision, was falling into puddles all the time; mud flew in cascades on all sides. Antonov and I were soon plastered with it. Thanks to the terrible darkness we lost our way and for a time wandered among the passageways of the fortress. I remember especially clearly one of the moments of this sad journey. Near one of the dimly flickering lanterns on the wall of the fortress Antonov suddenly stopped and inquiringly looked at me almost point-blank over his glasses. In his eyes I read suppressed alarm.

Now we were at the guns. Pavlov and Kondakov confirmed everything the artillerymen had said. Even by the light of the kerosene lamps they observed the severe rust on many parts of the guns and the lack of oil in the recoil mechanisms. Firing them was undoubtedly associated with tremendous risk. What to do? Could we find a comrade who knew how to fire the guns and would sacrifice his life for the revolution? (There were such comrades as was evident from later events.)

Somewhere far off the feet of a running man were splashing through the mud, closer and closer. We could hear him stumble and fall, let out a loud curse and the happy exclamation, "Comrade Blagonravov, where are you?" The voice gasped with joy. Intoxicating news: "The Winter Palace has surrendered and our men are there." Something big hit me in the head; it seemed like the ground was giving way under my feet; now the sleepless nights were telling on me too. Antonov gently supported me and squeezed my hand firmly. We went into the garrison club. The comrade who had been sent with the ultimatum a short time before had already returned and reported that he had carried out the assignment. However, the shooting did not stop, but I reassured myself with the thought that this was individual cadets holding out.

In the duty officer's room two sailors reported to me and presented me with a note signed by Comrade Lashevich to the effect that they were gunners and were placed at my disposal.

"It's pretty late now, comrades," I told them. "Now if you had arrived a couple of hours earlier, it would really have helped."

I told them the story of the guns. They said that although they were not specialists on field guns (sailors on the firing ranges—and these comrades were indeed from a firing range—chiefly learned to service fortress and naval guns), but nevertheless they felt that it would be possible to fire the three-inchers, allowing a certain risk.

I decided to go personally to the captured palace. Outwardly it was almost quiet. Only solitary shots rang out from time to time, and a blaze of fire cut the darkness of the night. I went out through the fortress gate. On the little bridge somebody's automobile clattered recklessly, blinding me with the light of its headlights. I approached closer and recognized Comrades Podvoisky and Yeremeyev. They were driving around among the units in the action and had stopped at the fortress to see how things were. I reported to them the news of the capture of the Winter Palace. We decided to drive together to the Winter Palace, and I got in the car.

We flew quickly over the Trinity Bridge, past the Champs de Mars, and along Millionaya Street toward the palace. On both sides soldiers of the Pavlov Regiment were scattered along the sidewalks, but closer to the bridge over the Winter Palace Canal we came upon a cordon of men stretched right across the street. They challenged us and held us up. We explained who we were. We conveyed the news of the capture of the Winter Palace. The news was met with great scepticism. A voice from the cordon exclaimed with authority, "Whether or not they've surrendered there, they gave us a healthy burn a while ago—it's dangerous to drive there." But we held to our opinion. We decided that the Winter Palace had been taken by units operating on the side of the Neva, and that the cordon had simply not been informed, and that the shooting which the comrade had spoken about referred to an earlier moment. We proceeded further. Behind us sounded a warning by our comrades to be careful. The driver reduced his speed. There was silence around us. Now the automobile had almost reached the arch of the Hermitage, and at that moment a loud "hurrah" rang out. A swarm of bullets whistled over the automobile, and several machine-guns began to fire wildly from the direction of the palace. Our driver, a plucky fellow, seeing that matters were taking a dangerous turn, stopped the car for an instant and shifted into reverse. Podvoisky and I dropped to the floor of the car so as not to be too big a target for the bullets, while Yeremeyev, who was sitting with the driver, jumped out onto the pavement and stretched out there according to all the rules of the military code. In a wink we flew back over the little bridge across the Winter Palace Canal and were out of danger, since the ground slopes down substantially beyond the bridge and the bullets could not hit us.

The fortunate ending of this episode is mainly explained by the fact that the cadets were poorly situated for longitudinal fire down Millionaya Street, and were very nervous, and especially because the driver was a man of tremendous self-possession.

The Pavlov men, alarmed by the heavy fire, the chattering of the machine-guns, the noise of the car and the shouts of "hurrah" which resounded from the direction of the palace, thought that an attack was being launched against them, and opened up with rapid and disorderly fire directed at the palace along Millionaya St., which created disarray among some groups of them, and they began to withdraw toward the Champs de Mars. Our situation was quite unenviable—we came under fire from both sides. We had to leave the car and shout out to the Pavlov men. The confusion was quickly liquidated. As it then became apparent, the report of the capture of the Winter Palace was false—only the headquarters building, situated on the Palace Square opposite the palace, had been captured.

We decided to open intensive fire immediately from the fortress. (I could promise to do this, since I remembered about the sailor-gunners who had been sent to me.) Immediately on my return I informed the sailors about the situation and what was demanded of them. At the same time I gave orders to open concentrated machine-gun fire along the embankment and at the palace. Soon the crackle of shooting told me that my order had been executed with dispatch. With the guns, too, everything was ready. The sailors had already loaded the guns and were waiting for the order to fire. A cordon under the command of Comrade Popel was placed along the bank to cover the guns (although it was hard to anticipate an attack by water and in boats).

When they received the order, without the slightest hesitation, the sailors opened a rapid fire on the palace. (I hasten to qualify this, in that of the 30 to 35 rounds shot off by them, hits were scored by only two—on the cornice of the Winter Palace—and a fragment of one shell went through a window and fell in the room inside, but no one was hurt. The other shots went high.) If the fire accomplished little damage, on the other hand it had a tremendous morale effect. The *Aurora* also spoke out with her guns. A real artillery battle began. The residents of the Winter Palace felt pretty unhappy. The fires in the courtyard had been put out long before, in order not to attract our attention and mark a target. From time to time a stray bullet whistled overhead. It went on this way for half an hour.

Chudnovsky reported by telephone the capture of the Winter Palace. Having been taught by bitter experience, I reacted to this report skeptically, but nevertheless I gave the order to cease fire for fear of shelling our own men. I made inquiries by telephone and received confirmation of the report of the capture of the Winter Palace. The joyful news quickly spread around the fortress. Antonov-Ovseyenko sent a note with the request to prepare cells in the Trubetskoy Bastion for the arrested ministers of the Provisional Government.

Through the night, under a strong guard of revolutionary workers and soldiers headed by Antonov, the historic procession of captured ministers entered the walls of the Peter-Paul Fortress. In the small hall of the garrison club, by the light of a smoky kerosene lamp (the electricity had failed), Antonov called the roll of the former personages. They sat sedately on the benches, while the dim rays flickered on their pale faces. How insignificant and pitiful they seemed among this crowd of workers and soldiers surrounding them. Blackened with mud and dust, but with flashing eyes and happy talk, the representatives of the insurrectionary nation stood proudly with rifles in their hands. What a striking contrast! A spectacle never to be repeated!

Antonov concluded all the formalities; the prisoners were led to their cells. Quietly the heavy door of the Trubetskoy Bastion closed on them. "That's the way for you," I heard one of our comrades exclaim. History, I thought, would say this. Happily I took leave of Antonov and hurried to my quarters in order first of all, after many sleepless nights, to get a few hours sleep.

The Siege of the Winter Palace: The Defenders

The defense of the Winter Palace by officer cadets and the "Women's Battalion of Death" was even more haphazard than the attack. The fall of the palace was described by P. I. Palchinsky, the commander of the defending forces, in notes made shortly after his capture—"The Last Days of the Provisional Government in 1917," *Krasny Arkhiv* [The Red Archive], no. 56 (1933), pp. 136–8. (Editor's translation.)

October 24

Evening in the Winter Palace. Business session. Talk with T., G. G., with Nikitin [Minister of the Interior] and Konovalov [Deputy Prime Minister]. Theoretical dispute, who is wrecking the revolution. Message about the telephone office. About 11:30 at Headquarters. Talk with Bagratuni [Chief of Staff of the military district] and Polkovnikov [Commander of the military district]. Malevsky is commissar. Personal merits, but not representation on the direct proposal of Polkovnikov. Obvious vacillation and fear on the part of the commissar of the CEC to take active part in any measures. Impotence of Polkovnikov and absence of any plan whatever. Hope that the crazy step will not be taken. No idea of what to do if it actually is. A look in at the Winter Palace and Kerensky in the hope of directives. My exposition of the hopelessness of the outlook. A mish-mash. No count of our forces and hopelessness of mood above all on the part of the commander, Rutenberg, P., P., and others. Explanation of the situation and unanimous evaluation. Plan for prompt implementation without Polkovnikov. Questions about his actions. No decision. P., Rutenberg, and I depart for home in view of the hopelessness of the leadership, around 2 A.M.

October 25

Called by Konovalov into the Winter Palace for a morning meeting. Suggestion of departure of Kerensky. Discussion of the general situation and its hopelessness. A soap bubble. Unanimity in evaluating the actions of Polkovnikov. Fruitlessness of discussion. Departed for defenses. Called to the Winter Palace by order of Kerensky around 1:30 P.M. Meeting. Wait in office. Events are unfolding. Departure of Kerensky. Meeting of the government. Rutenberg. His report. [To lead the defense] Government appoints Kishkin [Minister of Welfare] and me, and at my suggestion, Rutenberg. Decrees of the Provisional Government to remove Polkovnikov. Organization of the guard. Absence even of a diagram of the palace. Commandant Lieutenant Colonel Raetsky. Commander of one of the [officer cadet] schools—lazybones. Mikhailovsky School, three captains (Bratchikov, Yazev the second one). Explanation with the commanders of the units, the Cossacks, the Mikhailovsky School, the school of engineer officers, the Second Peterhof School and the Second Oranienbaum School. No provisions. No plan. Confusion and torpor of the officers and lack of morale among the cadets, for whom there was not enough concern. Measures adopted. Division of functions between Rutenberg and Palchinsky. Headquarters. Transmittal of orders. Last report of Polkovnikov. Before this, visit to Headquarters. Telegram to Supreme Headquarters. Held up at my insistence. Report to the Provisional Government on the telegram and the mood of Polkovnikov and Headquarters. All telegrams held up by Kishkin. Rumors of the resignation of all officials at Headquarters, confirmed afterwards, but Bagratuni did not report this.

Clarification of the provisioning question. At Headquarters enough for 700 men for 2½ days, in the Winter Palace nothing. Provisions already held up. Nothing new received. Tightening of the ring around the [Palace] Square. Cadets and shock troops begin to build barricades.

Report on the Mikhailovsky School. I called Captain Bratchikov. In reply, report that four guns had left and only two were retained. About 7 o'clock. I go to the Winter Palace. It is explained that the commandant heading the defense is Lieutenant Colonel Ananiev; the government commissar of the school led the Mikhailovsky cadets and the guns away. Departure of the last armored cars from the Square and from the Winter Palace. No gasoline at Headquarters or in the palace.

Report on the departure of schools [i.e., cadets]. Oranienbaum and Peterhof schools in the White Hall. Speech. Silence. Repeated appeal for performance of duty—shout: "We will!" (without enthusiasm and not all of them). Speech in the courtyard to the engineer cadets. "We will!"

Upstairs. Chudnovsky [the Bolshevik emissary] arrested. The Oranienbaum school changed their minds. The commander ap-

pears. Officers and cadets push in. Liberation of the arrested lieutenants Dashkevich and Chudnovsky separately. The school wants
to be covered by them when it moves out. My remarks on the danger
of moving out. (G. & M., adjutants, and the only real officers besides Sinegub and the shock trooper and Ananiev.) The school of
engineer officers has all this time been holding firm. Departure of
the Cossacks. Speech to them interrupted by the wounded. Speech
downstairs. Reports from the Duma [City Council], Prokopovich,
and the Central Committee of the Fleet. The schools do not leave,
but are agitated, it seems, and do almost nothing. Movement among
the barricades draws fire. We will leave, we will not leave, etc.
Break-ins by various stairways. Personally led engineer cadets in
disarming group of about 50 men who broke in through the Hermitage entrance. Surrender without resistance. Pavlov Regiment men
[Bolshevik] downstairs. All doors open. The servants let them in.
Slaves. The command too. The new arrivals lose their heads and
surrender their weapons to me alone. Report of Ananiev on negotiations. Chudnovsky again. Arrest him. Talk with the prisoners of
war. Release according to negotiations. Occupied below. Defense of
stairways and corridors. Sufficient numbers present for the defense,
if had officers and organization. Too late. No officers, spirit, or
provisions. Inform government of course of affairs. Disarm attackers.
Delegation from the city, peasant deputies under Prokopovich. Returning and departures every half hour. Determination to stay to
the end without surrendering. Rejection of ultimatums. Antonov
and Chudnovsky. Break-through upstairs. Decision not to fire. Refusal to negotiate. Go out to meet attackers. Antonov now in charge.
I am arrested by Antonov and Chudnovsky with declaration about
the governor-generalship. My explanations. Search. Defended by
Chudnovsky. Isolated. Guard of sailors. Nikitin next to me. On to
a room with all of us together. Protocol. Taken out. Critical moment. March. The bridge—the fortress. Documents. Signatures. Led
off to our cells. Margolin and others on guard. New point of view
for an anarchist.

Part Six

 THE CONSOLIDATION
OF SOVIET POWER

The Second Congress of Soviets, convening during the last hours of the Provisional Government on the evening of October 25th, was dominated by a majority of Bolsheviks and their Left SR allies. While most of the moderate socialists walked out in protest against the violent seizure of power, the remaining delegates proceeded to vote in the new Council of People's Commissars as the official government of Russia, and ratify a series of revolutionary decrees submitted by Lenin. Pro-Soviet forces quickly assumed control in most parts of Russia, while Kerensky vainly tried to organize a military counter-coup. Only in Moscow was there serious fighting before Soviet authority was established.

The future outlines of the Communist dictatorship quickly took shape in the next three months. A multitude of decrees were directed at the fundamental reform of society, and particularly of capitalist property rights. Sentiment for broadening the base of the regime to include all the parties of the soviets was quickly brushed aside by Lenin. The principle of suppressing all opposition by police terror was implicitly incorporated in the secret police, the Cheka. Finally, the Constituent Assembly, planned by the Provisional Government to determine Russia's political future, and elected democratically shortly after the Bolshevik coup, was closed down by the Soviet authorities after a one-day session in January, 1918. The Dictatorship of the Proletariat—in the minds of many critics a dictatorship over the Proletariat—had arrived.

The Soviet Government

The Second Congress of Soviets responded promptly to the overthrow of the Provisional Government by proclaiming the transfer of power to the soviets, and endorsing the assumption of executive power by a new cabinet, ostensibly temporary, termed the Council of People's Commissars.

a) Proclamation to the Workers, Soldiers and Peasants

The Second All-Russian Congress of Soviets of Workers' and Soldiers' Deputies has opened. The vast majority of the Soviets are represented at the Congress. A number of delegates from the Peasants' Soviets are also present. The mandate of the compromising Central Executive Committee has terminated. Backed by the will of the vast majority of the workers, soldiers and peasants, backed by the victorious uprising of the workers and the garrison which has taken place in Petrograd, the Congress takes the power into its own hands.

The Provisional Government has been overthrown. The majority of the members of the Provisional Government have already been arrested.

The Soviet government will propose an immediate democratic peace to all the nations and an immediate armistice on all fronts. It will secure the transfer of the land of the landlords, of the crown and monasteries to the peasants' committees without compensation; it will protect the rights of the soldiers by introducing complete democracy in the army; it will establish workers' control over production; it will ensure the convocation of the Constituent Assembly at the time appointed; it will see to it that bread is supplied to the cities and prime necessities to the villages; it will guarantee all the nations inhabiting Russia the genuine right of self-determination.

* Drafted by Lenin. (Translated in Lenin, *Selected Works*, vol. 2: part 1, pp. 326–7.)

The Congress decrees: all power in the localities shall pass to the Soviets of Workers', Soldiers' and Peasants' Deputies, which must guarantee genuine revolutionary order.

The Congress calls upon the soldiers in the trenches to be vigilant and firm. The Congress of Soviets is convinced that the revolutionary army will be able to defend the revolution against all attacks of imperialism until such time as the new government succeeds in concluding a democratic peace, which it will propose directly to all peoples. The new government will do everything to supply all the needs of the revolutionary army by means of a determined policy of requisitions and taxation of the propertied classes, and also will improve the condition of soldiers' families.

The Kornilovites—Kerensky, Kaledin and others—are attempting to bring troops against Petrograd. Several detachments, whom Kerensky had got to move by deceit, have come over to the side of the insurgent people.

Soldiers, actively resist Kerensky, the Kornilovite! Be on your guard!

Railwaymen, hold up all troop trains dispatched by Kerensky against Petrograd!

Soldiers, workers and employees, the fate of the revolution and the fate of the democratic peace is in your hands!

Long live the revolution!

b) *Decree on the Formation of a Workers' and Peasants' Government**

The All-Russian Congress of Soviets of Workers', Soldiers', and Peasants' Deputies decrees:

To form, for the administration of the country until the convocation of the Constituent Assembly, a provisional workers' and peasants' government, which will be called the Council of People's Commissars. The conduct of the particular branches of governmental activity is entrusted to commissions, whose make-up must guarantee the carrying out of the program proclaimed by the Congress, in close combination with the mass organizations of the workers, working women, sailors, soldiers, peasants, and white-

* Drafted by Lenin; published in Golikov, p. 432. (Editor's translation.)

collar workers. Governmental power is vested in the collegium of the representatives of these commissions, i.e., the Council of People's Commissars.

Control over the activity of the People's Commissars and the right to remove them are vested in the All-Russian Congress of Soviets of Workers', Peasants', and Soldiers' Deputies and its Central Executive Committee.

At the present time the Council of People's Commissars consists of the following persons:

Chairman of the Council—Vladimir Ulianov (Lenin)
People's Commissar for Internal Affairs—A. I. Rykov
Agriculture—V. P. Miliutin
Labor—A. G. Shliapnikov
For Military and Naval Affairs—a committee consisting of V. A. Ovseyenko (Antonov), N. V. Krylenko, and P. E. Dybenko.
For Commercial and Industrial Affairs—V. P. Nogin
Public Education—A. V. Lunarcharsky
Finance—I. I. Skvortsov (Stepanov)
For Foreign Affairs—L. D. Bronshtein (Trotsky)
Justice—G. I. Oppokov (Lomov)
For Food Supply—I. A. Teodorovich
Posts and Telegraphs—N. P. Avilov (Glebov)
Chairman for Nationality Affairs—I. V. Dzhugashvili (Stalin)

The post of People's Commissar for Railroad Affairs temporarily remains unfilled.

The Promises of Revolution

The aspirations of the soldiers for peace, of the peasants for land, of the national minorities for self-determination, and of the workers for control of the factories, were forthwith written into the revolutionary statute books by the Second Congress of Soviets and the Council of People's Commissars.

a) Decree on Peace, October 26, 1917*

The workers' and peasants' government created by the revolution of October 24–25 and relying on the Soviets of Workers', Soldiers' and Peasants' Deputies calls upon all the belligerent peoples and their governments to start immediate negotiations for a just, democratic peace.

By a just or democratic peace, for which the overwhelming majority of the working and toiling classes of all the belligerent countries, exhausted, tormented and racked by the war, are craving—a peace that has been most definitely and insistently demanded by the Russian workers and peasants ever since the overthrow of the tsarist monarchy—by such a peace the government means an immediate peace without annexations (i.e., without the seizure of foreign lands, without the forcible incorporation of foreign nations) and without indemnities.

This is the kind of peace the government of Russia proposes to all the belligerent nations to conclude immediately, and expresses its readiness to take all the resolute measures immediately, without the least delay, pending the final ratification of all the terms of such a peace by authoritative assemblies of the people's representatives of all countries and all nations.

In accordance with the sense of justice of the democracy in general, and of the toiling classes in particular, the government conceives the annexation or seizure of foreign lands to mean every incorporation into a large or powerful state of a small or weak nation without the precisely, clearly and voluntarily expressed consent and wish of that nation, irrespective also of the degree of development or backwardness of the nation forcibly annexed to, or forcibly retained within, the borders of the given state, and irrespective, finally, of whether this nation resides in Europe or in distant, overseas countries.

If any nation whatsoever is forcibly retained within the borders of a given state, if, in spite of its expressed desire—no matter whether expressed in the press, at public meetings, in the decisions

---

* Drafted by Lenin. (Translated in Lenin, *Selected Works*, vol. 2: part 1, pp. 328–31.)

of parties, or in protests and uprisings against national oppression —it is not accorded the right to decide the forms of its state existence by a free vote, taken after the complete evacuation of the troops of the incorporating or, generally, of the stronger nation and without the least pressure being brought to bear, such incorporation is annexation, i.e., seizure and violence.

The government considers it the greatest of crimes against humanity to continue this war over the issue of how to divide among the strong and rich nations the weak nationalities they have conquered, and solemnly announces its determination immediately to sign terms of peace to stop this war on the conditions indicated, which are equally just for all nationalities without exception.

At the same time the government declares that it does not regard the above-mentioned terms of peace as an ultimatum; in other words, it is prepared to consider any other terms of peace, but only insists that they be advanced by any of the belligerent nations as speedily as possible, and that in the proposals of peace there should be absolute clarity and the complete absence of all ambiguity and secrecy.

The government abolishes secret diplomacy, and, for its part, announces its firm intention to conduct all negotiations quite openly under the eyes of the whole people. It will immediately proceed to the full publication of the secret treaties endorsed or concluded by the government of landlords and capitalists from February to October 25, 1917. The government proclaims the absolute and immediate annulment of everything contained in these secret treaties in so far as it is aimed, as is mostly the case, at securing advantages and privileges for the Russian landlords and capitalists and at the retention, or extension, of the annexations made by the Great Russians.

Proposing to the governments and peoples of all countries immediately to begin open negotiations for peace, the government, for its part, expresses its readiness to conduct these negotiations both in writing, by telegraph, and by negotiations between representatives of the various countries, or at a conference of such representatives. In order to facilitate such negotiations, the government is appointing its plenipotentiary representative to neutral countries.

The government proposes an immediate armistice to the governments and peoples of all the belligerent countries, and, for its part, considers it desirable that this armistice should be concluded for a period of not less than three months, i.e., a period long enough to permit the completion of negotiations for peace with the participation of the representatives of all peoples or nations, without exception, involved in or compelled to take part in the war and the summoning of authoritative assemblies of the representatives of the peoples of all countries for the final ratification of the terms of peace.

While addressing this proposal for peace to the governments and peoples of all the belligerent countries, the Provisional Workers' and Peasants' Government of Russia appeals in particular also to the class-conscious workers of the three most advanced nations of mankind and the largest states participating in the present war, namely, Great Britain, France and Germany. The workers of these countries have made the greatest contributions to the cause of progress and Socialism; they have furnished the great examples of the Chartist movement in England, a number of revolutions of historic importance effected by the French proletariat, and, finally, the heroic struggle against the Anti-Socialist Law in Germany and the prolonged, persistent and disciplined work of creating mass proletarian organizations in Germany, a work which serves as a model to the workers of the whole world. All these examples of proletarian heroism and historic creative work are a pledge that the workers of the countries mentioned will understand the duty that now faces them of saving mankind from the horrors of war and its consequences, that these workers, by comprehensive, determined, and supremely vigorous action, will help us to bring to a successful conclusion the cause of peace, and at the same time the cause of the emancipation of the toiling and exploited masses of the population from all forms of slavery and all forms of exploitation.

b) Decree on the Land, October 26, 1917*

1. Landlord ownership of land is abolished forthwith without any compensation.

2. The landed estates, as also all crown, monastery and church lands, with all their livestock, implements, buildings and everything pertaining thereto, shall be placed at the disposal of the volost

---

* Drafted by Lenin. (Translated in Lenin, *Selected Works*, vol. 2: part 1, pp. 339–42.)

Land Committees and the uyezd Soviets of Peasants' Deputies pending the convocation of the Constituent Assembly.

3. All damage to confiscated property, which henceforth belongs to the whole people, is proclaimed a grave crime to be punished by the revolutionary courts. The uyezd Soviets of Peasants' Deputies shall take all necessary measures to assure the observance of the strict order during the confiscation of the landed estates, to determine the size of the estates, and the particular estates subject to confiscation, to draw up exact inventories of all property confiscated and to protect in a strict revolutionary way all agricultural enterprises transferred to the people, with all buildings, implements, livestock, produce stocks, etc.

4. The following peasant Mandate, compiled by the *Izvestia of the All-Russian Soviet of Peasants' Deputies* from 242 local peasant mandates and published in No. 88 of the *Izvestia* (Petrograd, No. 88, August 19, 1917), shall serve everywhere to guide the implementation of the great land reforms until a final decision on the latter is taken by the Constituent Assembly.

5. The land of ordinary peasants and ordinary Cossacks shall not be confiscated.

PEASANT MANDATE ON THE LAND

The land question in its full scope can be settled only by the popular Constituent Assembly.

The most equitable settlement of the land question is to be as follows:

1. *Private ownership of land shall be abolished forever;* land shall not be sold, purchased, leased, mortgaged, or otherwise alienated.

All land, whether *state, appanage, crown, monastery, church, factory, primogenitary, private, public, peasant, etc., shall be alienated without compensation* and become the property of the whole people, and pass into the use of all those who cultivate it.

Persons who suffer by this property revolution shall be deemed to be entitled to public support only for the period necessary for adaptation to the new conditions of life.

2. All mineral wealth, e.g., ore, oil, coal, salt, etc., as well as all forests and waters of state importance, shall pass into the exclusive use of the state. All the small streams, lakes, woods, etc., shall pass into the use of the communities, to be administered by the local self-government bodies.

3. Lands on which *high-level scientific* farming is practised, e.g., orchards, plantations, seed plots, nurseries, hothouses, etc., *shall not*

be divided up, but shall be converted into model farms, to be turned over for exclusive use *to the state or to the communities,* depending on the size and importance of such lands.

Household land in towns and villages, with orchards and vegetable gardens shall be reserved for the use of their present owners, the size of the holdings, and the size of the tax levied for the use thereof, to be determined by law.

4. Stud farms, government and private pedigree stock and poultry farms, etc., shall be confiscated and become the property of the whole people, to pass into the exclusive use of the state or of the communities, depending on the size and importance of such farms.

The question of compensation shall be examined by the Constituent Assembly.

5. All livestock and farm implements of the confiscated estates shall pass into the exclusive use of the state or a community, depending on their size and importance, and no compensation shall be paid for this.

The farm implements of peasants with little land shall not be subject to confiscation.

6. The right to use the land shall be accorded to all citizens of the Russian state (without distinction of sex) desiring to cultivate it by their own labour, with the help of their families, or in partnership, but only as long as they are able to cultivate it. The employment of hired labour is not permitted.

In the event of the temporary physical disability of any member of a village community for a period of up to two years, the village community shall be obliged to assist him for this period by collectively cultivating his land until he is again able to work.

Peasants who, owing to old age or ill-health, are permanently disabled and unable to cultivate the land personally, shall lose their right to the use of it, but, in return, shall receive a pension from the state.

7. Land tenure shall be on an equality basis, i.e., the land shall be distributed among the toilers in conformity with a labour standard or a consumption standard, depending on local conditions.

There shall be absolutely no restriction on the forms of land tenure: household, farm, communal, or cooperative, as shall be decided in each individual village and settlement.

8. All land, when alienated, shall become part of the national land fund. Its distribution among the toilers shall be in charge of the local and central self-government bodies, from democratically organized village and city communities, in which there are no distinctions of social rank, to central regional government bodies.

The land fund shall be subject to periodical redistribution, depending on the growth of population and the increase in the productivity and the scientific level of farming.

When the boundaries of allotments are altered, the original nucleus of the allotment shall be left intact.

The land of the members who leave the community shall revert to the land fund; preferential right to such land shall be given to the near relatives of the members who have left, or to persons designated by the latter.

The cost of fertilizers and improvements put into the land, to the extent that they have not been fully used up at the time an allotment is returned to the land fund, shall be compensated.

Should the available land fund in a particular district prove inadequate for the needs of the local population, the surplus population shall be settled elsewhere.

The state shall take upon itself the organization of resettlement and shall bear the cost thereof, as well as the cost of supplying implements, etc.

Resettlement shall be effected in the following order: landless peasants desiring to resettle, then members of the community who are of vicious habits, deserters, and so on, and, finally, by lot or by agreement.

The entire contents of this mandate, as expressing the absolute will of the vast majority of the class-conscious peasants of all Russia, are proclaimed a provisional law, which, pending the convocation of the Constituent Assembly, shall be carried into effect as far as possible immediately, and as to certain of its provisions with due gradualness, as shall be determined by the uyezd Soviets of Peasants' Deputies.

c) Decree of the Council of People's Commissars, November 2, 1917, "On the Rights of the Peoples of Russia to Self-Determination" *

The November revolution of the workers and peasants began under the common banner of emancipation.

The peasants are being emancipated from the power of the landlords, for the landlord no longer has any property right in the land —that right has been abolished. The soldiers and sailors are being emancipated from the power of autocratic generals, for henceforth

* Translated in Bunyan and Fisher, *The Bolshevik Revolution*, pp. 282–3.

generals will be elective and subject to recall. The workers are being emancipated from the whims and arbitrary will of the capitalists, for henceforth workers' control will be established over mills and factories. Everything living and viable is being emancipated from hateful shackles.

There remain now only the peoples of Russia who have suffered and are suffering under an arbitrary yoke. Their emancipation must be considered at once and their liberation effected with resoluteness and finality.

During the tsarist times the peoples of Russia were systematically incited against one another. The results of this policy are well known: massacres and pogroms on the one hand, slavery and bondage on the other.

There can be and there must be no return to this shameful policy of provocation. Henceforth it must be replaced by a policy of voluntary and honest co-operation of the people of Russia.

During the period of imperialism, after the March Revolution, when the government passed into the hands of [the] Kadet bourgeoisie, the unconcealed policy of instigation gave way to one of cowardly distrust of the peoples of Russia, of caviling and provocation camouflaged by verbal declarations about the "freedom" and "equality" of peoples. The results of this policy, too, are well known —the growth of national enmity, the impairment of mutual trust.

An end must be made to this unworthy policy of falsehood and distrust, of cavil and provocation. Henceforth it must be replaced by an open and honest policy leading to complete mutual confidence among the peoples of Russia.

Only as the result of such a confidence can an honest and lasting union of the peoples of Russia be formed.

Only as the result of such a union can the workers and peasants of the peoples of Russia be welded into a revolutionary force capable of resisting all [counter-revolutionary] attempts on the part of the imperialist-annexationist bourgeoisie.

The Congress of Soviets, in June of this year, proclaimed the right of the peoples of Russia to free self-determination.

The Second Congress of Soviets, in November [October, old style] of this year, reaffirmed this inalienable right of the peoples of Russia more decisively and definitely.

In compliance with the will of these Congresses, the Soviet [Council] of People's Commissars has resolved to adopt as the basis of its activity on the problem of nationalities in Russia the following principles:

1. Equality and sovereignty of the peoples of Russia.
2. The right to free self-determination of peoples even to the point of separating and forming independent states.
3. Abolition of each and every privilege or limitation based on nationality or religion.
4. Free development of national minorities and ethnographic groups inhabiting Russian territory.

All concrete measures appertaining to the above declaration are to be decreed immediately upon the formation of a special commission for nationalities.

IOSIF DZHUGASHVILI (STALIN)
Commissar for Nationalities

V. ULIANOV (LENIN)
President of Soviet
of People's Commissars

d) *Decree of the Council of People's Commissars, November 14, 1917, "On Workers' Control"* *

1. In the interests of a systematic regulation of national economy, Workers' Control is introduced in all industrial, commercial, agricultural [and similar] enterprises which are hiring people to work for them in their shops or which are giving them work to take home. This control is to extend over the production, storing, buying and selling of raw materials and finished products as well as over the finances of the enterprise.

2. The workers will exercise this control through their elected organizations, such as factory and shop committees, Soviets of elders, etc. The office employees and the technical personnel are also to have representation in these committees.

3. Every large city, gubernia, and industrial area is to have its own Soviet of Workers' Control, which, being an organ of the S[oviet] of W[orkers'], S[oldiers'], and P[easants'] D[eputies], must be composed of representatives of trade-union, factory, shop and other workers' committees and workers' co-operatives.

4. Until the meeting of the Congress of the Soviets of Workers'

* Translated in Bunyan and Fisher, *The Bolshevik Revolution,* pp. 308–10.

Control an All-Russian Soviet of Workers' Control will be organized in Petrograd, made up of representatives from the following organizations: All-Russian Central Executive Committee of the Soviet of Workers' and Soldiers' Deputies (5 [representatives]); All-Russian Central Executive Committee of the Soviet of Peasant Deputies (5); All-Russian Council of Trade Unions (5); All-Russian Union of Workers' Co-operatives (2); All-Russian Bureau of Factory and Shop Committees (5); All-Russian Union of Engineers and Technicians (5); All-Russian Union of Agronomists (2); from every All-Russian union of workers having less than 100,000 members (1); from those that have more than 100,000 members (2); the Petrograd Council of Trade Unions (2).

5. Commissions of trained inspectors (technicians, accountants, etc.) will be established in connection with the higher organs of Workers' Control and will be sent out either on the initiative of these higher organs or at the request of the lower organs of Workers' Control to investigate the financial and technical side of enterprises.

6. The organs of Workers' Control have the right to supervise production, fix the minimum of output, and determine the cost of production.

7. The organs of Workers' Control have the right to control all the business correspondence of an enterprise. Owners of enterprises are legally responsible for all correspondence kept secret. Commercial secrets are abolished. The owners have to show to the organs of Workers' Control all their books and statements for the current year and for past years.

8. The rulings of the organs of Workers' Control are binding on the owners of enterprises and can be annulled only by decisions of the higher organs of Workers' Control.

9. Appeals from the lower to the higher organs must be made within three days.

10. In all enterprises the owners and the representatives of the workers and employees elected to the Committee on Workers' Control are responsible to the state for the order, discipline, and safety of the property. Persons guilty of hiding raw materials or products, of falsifying accounts, and other similar abuses are criminally liable.

11. All regional Soviets of Workers' Control (Article 3) have the power to settle disputed points and conflicts that may arise between the lower organs of the Workers' Control and to give their decision regarding the complaints of the owners. They also issue instructions (within the limits fixed by the All-Russian Soviet of

Workers' Control) to meet the local conditions of production and supervise the activities of the lower organs of control.

12. The All-Russian Soviet of Workers' Control makes out a general plan for Workers' Control, issues instructions, makes binding decisions, regulates mutual relations between the different Soviets of Workers' Control, and serves as the highest authority for all business connected with Workers' Control.

13. The All-Russian Soviet of Workers' Control coordinates the activities of the organs of Workers' Control in their dealings with other institutions of national economy.

Special instructions will be issued later defining the relations between the All-Russian Soviet of Workers' Control and other institutions of national economy.

14. All the laws and circulars restricting the work of factory, shop, and other committees or Soviets of workers and employees are hereby annulled.

V. Ulianov (Lenin)
President of the Soviet
of People's Commissars

A. Shliapnikov
People's Commissar of Labor

Lenin on Party Dictatorship

Following the Bolshevik seizure of power the Mensheviks and SRs negotiated with the victors regarding a coalition government, but stipulated that Lenin and Trotsky be excluded from the cabinet. The same Bolshevik elements who opposed the insurrection urged acceptance of these terms for coalition in order to avoid civil war. Lenin responded with an angry defense of the Bolsheviks' right to rule. His "Statement from the Central Committee of the Russian Social-Democratic Workers' Party (Bolsheviks), to All Party Members and to All the Toiling Classes of Russia," is translated in Lenin, *Selected Works*, vol. 2: part 1, pp. 346–8, 350–1.

Comrades,

It is a matter of common knowledge that the majority at the Second All-Russian Congress of Soviets of Workers' and Soldiers' Deputies consisted of delegates belonging to the Bolshevik Party.

This fact is fundamental for a proper understanding of the victorious revolution that has just taken place in Petrograd, Moscow and the whole of Russia. Yet this fact is constantly forgotten and ignored by all the supporters of the capitalists and their unwitting aides, who are undermining the fundamental principle of the new revolution, namely *all power to the Soviets*. There must be no government in Russia other than the *Soviet government*. The Soviet power has been won in Russia, and the transfer of government from one Soviet party to another is guaranteed without any revolution, simply by a decision of the Soviets, simply by new elections of deputies to the Soviets. The majority at the Second All-Russian Congress of Soviets belongs to the Bolshevik Party. Therefore only a government formed by that party will be a Soviet government. And everybody knows that the Central Committee of the Bolshevik Party, several hours prior to the formation of the new government, and [prior] to the presentation of the list of its members to the Second All-Russian Congress of Soviets, summoned to its session three of the most prominent members of the group of Left Socialist-Revolutionaries, Comrades Kamkov, Spiro and Karelin, and invited them to join the new government. We extremely regret that the Left Socialist-Revolutionary comrades refused; we regard their refusal as impermissible on the part of revolutionaries and champions of the toilers. We are ready at any moment to include Left Socialist-Revolutionaries in the government, but we declare that, as the majority party at the Second All-Russian Congress of Soviets, we are entitled to form the government, *and it is our duty* to the people to do so.

Everybody knows that the Central Committee of our party submitted a purely Bolshevik list of People's Commissars to the Second All-Russian Congress of Soviets, and that *the Congress approved this list of a purely Bolshevik government.*

Hence the statements to the effect that the Bolshevik government is *not* a Soviet government are absolute lies, and come, and can come, only from the enemies of the people, from the enemies of the Soviet power. On the contrary, now, after the Second All-Russian Congress of Soviets, and until the Third Congress meets, or until new elections to the Soviets are held, or until a new government is formed by the Central Executive Committee, *only* a Bolshevik government can be regarded as the *Soviet* government.

Comrades, yesterday, November 4, several members of the Central Committee of our Party and of the Council of People's Commissars—Kamenev, Zinoviev, Nogin, Rykov, Miliutin and a few others—resigned from the Central Committee of our Party, and the three last named from the Council of People's Commissars. In a large party like ours, notwithstanding the proletarian and revolutionary line of our policy, it was inevitable that individual comrades should have proven to be insufficiently staunch and firm in the struggle against the enemies of the people. The tasks that now face our Party are truly immense, the difficulties are enormous, and several members of our Party who formerly occupied responsible posts have flinched in face of the onslaught of the bourgeoisie and fled from our ranks. The bourgeoisie and all its helpers are jubilant over the fact and are maliciously rejoicing, clamouring about disintegration and predicting the fall of the Bolshevik government.

Comrades, do not believe these lies. The comrades who have resigned have acted like deserters, since they not only quitted the posts entrusted to them, but violated the direct decision of the Central Committee of our Party binding them to delay their resignation at least until a decision be taken by the Petrograd and Moscow Party organizations. We vigorously condemn this desertion. We are profoundly convinced that all class-conscious workers, soldiers and peasants who belong to or sympathize with our Party will condemn the actions of the deserters with equal vigour.

But we declare that not for one minute, and not in one iota, can the desertion of several individuals belonging to the leading group of our Party shake the unity of the masses who support our Party, and that it therefore will not shake our Party. . . .

The gentlemen who stand behind the Left Socialist-Revolutionaries and act through them in the interests of the bourgeoisie interpreted our readiness to make concessions as weakness and took advantage of this readiness to present us with new ultimatums. At the conference on November 3 Messrs. Abramovich and Martov [Mensheviks] appeared and presented an ultimatum: no negotiations until our government puts a stop to the arrests and to the suppression of bourgeois newspapers.

Both our Party and the General Executive Committee of the Congress of Soviets *refused* to accept this ultimatum, which obviously emanated from the supporters of Kaledin, the bourgeoisie, Kerensky and Kornilov. The conspiracy of Purishkevich and the appearance in Petrograd on November 5 of a delegation from a unit of the 17th Army Corps threatening us with a march on Petrograd (a ridiculous threat, for the advance detachments of these Kornilovites have already been beaten and have taken to flight at

Gatchina, while most of them have refused to fight against the Soviets)—all these events have proved who were the real authors of the ultimatum of Messrs. Abramovich and Martov and whom these people *really* served.

Let the toilers, therefore, keep calm and firm! Never will our Party yield to the ultimatums of the minority in the Soviets, the minority which has allowed itself to be intimidated by the bourgeoisie and which despite its "good intentions" virtually acts as a puppet in the hands of the Kornilovites.

We stand firmly by the principle of the Soviet power, i.e., the power of the *majority* obtained at the last Congress of Soviets. We agreed and *still agree,* to share the power with the minority of the Soviets, provided that minority loyally and honestly undertakes to submit to the majority and carry out the program *approved by the whole* Second All-Russian Congress of Soviets, providing for gradual, but firm and undeviating steps towards Socialism. But we will not submit to any ultimatums of groups of intellectuals who are not backed by the masses, and who *in actual fact* are backed only by the Kornilovites, the Savinkovites,[1] the Kadets, etc.

Let all the toilers, therefore, keep calm and firm! Our Party, the party of the Soviet majority, stands solid and united in defence of their interests and, as heretofore, behind our Party stand the millions of the workers in the cities, the soldiers in the trenches and the peasants in the villages, prepared at all costs to achieve the victory of peace and the victory of Socialism!

Resistance Begins: Moscow

Throughout Russia there was initially little effective resistance to the Bolsheviks' seizure of power in the name of the soviets, except in Moscow. The week of bitter fighting there between the Soviet forces and the military authorities, presaging the three-year ordeal of civil war that lay ahead for the peoples of Russia, was graphically recounted in the memoirs of two of the Bolshevik participants.

[1] [Referring to Kerensky's Deputy Minister of War—ED.]

a) Y. Y. Peche's Account*

. . . During the night of November 7–8 (October 25–26) the leaders of the Red Guard of the Khamovnichesky district came to Red Guard Headquarters to discuss the question of sending a unit of Red Guards under the leadership of experienced party comrades into the Kremlin to propagandize the military units remaining there who had not chosen either side.

The Red Guards were in communication with representatives of the 56th Regiment stationed in the Kremlin. It was decided to move into the Kremlin arsenal partly in trucks, and partly through the gates and walls where the sentries of the 56th Regiment admitted our Red Guards.

On entering the Kremlin, these Red Guards under the leadership of Comrade Strakhov began to carry on conversations in groups. Then, after they held a general meeting, they decided to get weapons from the Kremlin arsenal for the Red Guard. . . .

Events developed rapidly.

The morning of November 8 (October 26) the cadets began firing on the Moscow Soviet and Skobelevskaya (now Sovietskaya) Square with machine guns. This was the beginning of the decisive armed clash of the Revolution with the forces of bourgeois reaction.

On November 8 (October 26) the Red Guard was brought to full combat readiness. . . .

On November 10 (October 28) and especially on November 11 (October 29) the fighting was very bitter. The enemy held on with extraordinary firmness. On November 11 (October 29), especially in the center of the city, the enemy obviously did not think of surrendering. But contrary to all expectations we suddenly received a proposal for a cease-fire. The cease-fire was nevertheless concluded. This was one of the greatest mistakes of the Military Revolutionary Committee, since the Whites at that point were in a very difficult situation and were cut off by us from all their central and local bases of munitions. In our hands were all the arms depots and arsenals with the exception of the Kremlin, which remained in the

---

* "The Struggle of the Red Guard in Moscow," *Proletarskaya Revoliutsiya*, no. 70 (1927), pp. 177–78. (Editor's translation.)

hands of the enemy.[1] All transportation was also in our hands. We denied our enemies the possibility of redeploying their units and supplying them with munitions. The enemy had an extremely large quantity of shells, cartridges, and hand grenades. But by our energetic pressure from the outlying districts we barred the way to these stores. Thus the enemy was left without military supplies, and for this and other reasons proposed a cease-fire on November 11 (October 29).

At that point the counter-revolutionaries hoped to win time in the expectation of reinforcements. Cossack regiments were coming from the south, and shock troops on the Bryansk railroad.

For them the cease-fire was a breathing spell which they proposed to use to strengthen their forces. . . .

b) B. Berzin's Account*

. . . It is now 10 or 11 o'clock in the morning [on October 26]. The situation is rather strange: we hold the Kremlin, around the Kremlin are the cadets; neither the one side nor the other begins military action. They wait. What is going on in the districts and among the other units of the garrison is not known. It is bad that we did not succeed in getting weapons out [of the Kremlin]: in the districts there are few weapons, and the majority of the Moscow regiments are poorly armed. I call the Military-Revolutionary Committee, and report that the Kremlin is surrounded by cadets, and we have not gotten the weapons out. They ask me what the mood is; I report that Riabtsev[2] insists that we admit several companies of cadets into the Kremlin, because he is afraid that the Kremlin might be pillaged, etc. I answered that our mood is good, that the 56th Regiment has always guarded the Kremlin; if they bring the cadets in here, it will be an expression of non-confidence in the soldiers of the 56th Regiment. . . .

---

[1] [Actually the Kremlin had just been surrendered to the anti-Bolshevik forces that morning; cf. selection (b)—ED.]

* "The October Days in Moscow," *Proletarskaya Revoliutsiya*, no. 71 (1927), pp. 177–83. (Editor's translation.)

[2] [Colonel in command of the anti-Bolshevik forces—ED.]

It is now noon. The situation is indeterminate. There have been no clear preparations to take decisive measures without stopping halfway and proceeding to arrest all the officers without exception. Therefore there has been a fear of overdoing it. We have not received any directive to open fire.

Suddenly through the Troitsky Gate come Comrade Muralov, Colonel Riabtsev, Comrade Nogin, Comrade Blokhin from the Soviet of Soldiers' Deputies, and someone else, Stukov I think.

We call a meeting right here on the square in front of the barracks. Colonel Riabtsev speaks. He says that the vaults of the Kremlin contain the whole Russian gold reserve and many other valuables, that the 56th Regiment is tired, and the guarding of the Kremlin needs to be entrusted to the cadets. Right here the soldiers yell at him: "Down with him! To the devil! We've always guarded the Kremlin. Don't let the cadets into the Kremlin! Enough!" They almost beat Riabtsev up. Muralov assured Riabtsev: "Now see here: I told you that the 56th Regiment won't leave; there is no reason why you should bring the cadets in."

Here Comrade Yaroslavsky spoke up briefly, if I am correct, and said let Colonel Riabtsev leave but the 56th Regiment would not let the cadets into the Kremlin.

Riabtsev, Muralov, Yaroslavsky and the others all together went out of the Kremlin through the Troitsky Gate.

The rest of the day went by quietly until evening. In the evening, after dark, some shooting was heard on the Red Square side—rifle and machine gun fire. Who was shooting, and whom they were shooting at was not known. I did not give the order to open fire. Later on it appeared that this was the skirmish of the Dvina Unit, moving through Red Square, with the cadets. Then it became quiet. After some time shooting began again somewhere. I climbed upon the Kremlin wall near the Spassky Tower. Several rounds from a gun sounded; several shells exploded over the Kremlin; shrapnel pellets were sprayed on the iron roofs of the buildings. It was impossible to figure out who was shooting and from where. Soon everything quieted down. Only at times distant rifle and machine gun fire was heard in the city.

During the evening of November 9 (October 27) I spoke several times by telephone with the Military Revolutionary Committee. They informed me that the 55th Regiment was moving into the center of the city from the Zamoskvorechie district, while the 255th was going towards Lubianka Square and we were to let it into the Kremlin to strengthen the Kremlin garrison. The second time—it was already around midnight—they informed me that the 1st Artillery Brigade had been given the assignment to send some guns immediately to Red Square for my disposal. After this I had no more conversations with the MRC. The Central telephone exchange did not answer. Apparently the wires had been cut. I lost contact. In various directions shooting was reported; where it originated was hard to tell. In anticipation of the arrival of units of the 255th Regiment and the Artillery I patrolled the posts all night. I had the keys to the Kremlin gates on me.

During the night it was reported to me that the cadets were not visible below the walls of the Kremlin; apparently they had left.

The night was an anxious one, all anticipation.

Around four o'clock some soldiers ran up to me and in a rather abrupt form demanded that I go right then to the barracks, because a meeting in the quarters of the 2nd Company demanded me. I ask what kind of a special meeting at night, since I had been in the barracks not long before and the people were asleep. What happened? I go in. In the quarters of the 2nd Company an impromptu meeting has gathered. Staff Sergeant Ivanov of the 3rd Company (an SR) is speaking, and argues that I have deceived the soldiers, that I have betrayed them. Ivanov is followed by the Commander of the 2nd Company, Sub-lieutenant Maltsev (an SR), who asserts that they are beating the Bolsheviks in the city, that artillery is trained on the Kremlin and that in an hour they will begin to shell the Kremlin; whoever does not want to perish should throw down his arms and leave the Kremlin.

I see that the mood is wound up to the highest degree.

I must say that among the companies of the 56th Regiment stationed in the Kremlin, aside from me there was not one Bolshevik (SRs were the usual). . . . The situation was critical. . . .

On November 10 (October 28) at daybreak the cadets again surrounded the Kremlin. The shooting in the city gradually began to quiet down. I had no kind of communication with anyone. No one knew what was happening in the city. The promised units did not arrive. The cadets are around the Kremlin again.

The soldiers ask how long we will remain without news; aren't the Whites taking the lead? . . .

About six o'clock in the morning [on October 29] a soldier from the armored car crew comes and informs me that I am wanted on the telephone right away. I was quite surprised, because for more than twenty-four hours I had had no communication with the city, not even by telephone. They want me at the telephone situated in the quarters of the armored car crew. Strange—their telephone works, mine doesn't.

I go past the barracks, turn the corner, and see both armored cars standing in the street with their motors running; in each armored car are a cannon and three machine guns. I feel that something is wrong. I go into the crew's quarters. An officer meets me, hands me the receiver, and says, "The commander of the troops wants you." I take the receiver and listen. The commander of the troops, Riabtsev, speaks: "All units which have rebelled have been disarmed, including the First Artillery Brigade. I demand the immediate surrender of the Kremlin. Soldiers who voluntarily lay down their arms are guaranteed freedom." To my answer that I knew nothing of this and that I was subordinate only to the Military-Revolutionary Committee, Riabtsev declared: "The whole city is in my hands. All members of the MRC have been arrested. I give you twenty-five minutes to surrender. In case of noncompliance I will open artillery fire."

All external circumstances—the complete absence of communication with the directing center, the quiet in the city—I had not heard shooting since lunch the day before—the night that had passed quietly—the non-arrival of the reinforcements promised by the MRC—all this made me think that Riabtsev was telling the truth.

This means that all is lost. If all the remaining units have been disarmed, what sense is there in holding the Kremlin alone? It means that the shooting I heard yesterday before lunch and the day before yesterday ceased because the uprising was put down; the 255th Regiment and the 1st Artillery Brigade did not reach us because they had been disarmed.

Since I did not calculate that the isolated forces of the Kremlin garrison alone could operate successfully, I decided to surrender the Kremlin, in order to spare the soldiers from shooting and avoid senseless bloodshed. I was then still young and naive enough to rely on the magnanimity of the victor—of course, as regards myself, an officer in charge of a unit in rebellion, I did not expect mercy—I relied on magnanimity in regards to the soldiers. Subsequent events showed that I was sadly mistaken.

I answered Riabtsev that I would submit to his order if he promised me to spare the soldiers, who were not guilty of anything, since all responsibility rested on me, and I alone would answer for everything.

Riabtsev promised complete impartiality toward soldiers who voluntarily laid down their arms. . . .

. . . Approaching the soldiers, I explained the state of things to them and said that I had to surrender the Kremlin. One of the soldiers with a face distorted by fright shouted at me, "Ah, traitor!" and threw himself at me with his rifle. I calmly said to him, "Shoot, shoot!" and repeated this request once more. The soldier emptied the rifle, threw it down, held his head, and left. The rest also left their posts and threw down their arms.

I went to the Borovitsky Gate and opened it. Not far away stood the cadets with their rifles at the ready, with machine guns and one cannon. I went to meet them. I was still at a distance when they shouted, "Drop your weapons!" Two officers ran up and took away my cartridges, a third took away my holster and tore out the revolver, and someone hit me several times in the face. Seeing their commander, some lieutenant-general, I told him that I had not yet removed all the guards and asked him not to let the cadets into the Kremlin. I went back into the Kremlin surrounded by officers and cadets. Some naval officer hopped over and threw himself at me, "Ah, a Bolshevik! You've been shooting us in Petrograd," and began to beat me. I fell. As I got up I again asked them to avoid superfluous bloodshed, to give me a chance to remove the sentries from the Nikolsky and Spassky Gates. At the Spassky Gate shooting began, and on the Senate Square several machine guns rattled. They assigned three cadets and an officer as my guard. Merciless shooting began, machine-gun fire. When they brought me to the Senate Square I saw at the gate of the arsenal several dozen corpses and severely wounded soldiers, and spots of blood around on the pavement. It appears that the cadets and officers fired with a machine gun into the disarmed soldiers lined up in two ranks. Many died. Sub-lieutenant Pshenitsyn of our 8th Company broke into a run as soon as the machine gun began to chatter, and jumped into a window, but a bullet caught him, and his massive body hung on the window sill. . . .

c) *Peche's Account Continued* *

. . . When the complete ineffectiveness of the leadership of the Military-Revolutionary Committee became clear, the Leninist

* *Loc cit.*, pp. 180–181.

portion of the MRC headed by Comrades Bukharin, Olminsky, et al., moved into the building of the former Commercial Institute and from there directed the coup.

The offensive of the Whites [after the cease-fire ended] was quickly checked, and by November 13 (October 31) our forces with the adherence of all the revolutionary units of the garrison had grown to approximately 100,000. Then they increased with each passing day, so that by the end of the uprising, on November 15th (2nd), they amounted to 200,000 men.

The development of the fight facilitated the pace of a vast upsurge of revolutionary feeling, which embraced even the soldiers of the old army who had taken a passive attitude up to this time, and all the rest of the workers who at the beginning had not joined in the decisive armed struggle. This upsurge of the broadest strata of workers and soldiers played a great role in the final victory of the proletariat.

We had surrounded the Whites on all sides and pressed them in a ring which was gradually tightened. By the 14th (1st) and 15th (2nd) of November only the Kremlin, the Alexandrovsky Military School and the Arbat district remained in their hands. Their lot was decided. The Whites again resorted to a cease-fire.

The adoption of the cease-fire was received by the worker and soldier masses with great hostility.

Comrade Smidovich and some other members of the Moscow Committee, seeing the mood of the masses, went out to the districts for the purpose of calming them, but they did not succeed in convincing the masses, and it was decided to send me with a detachment to take the Kremlin by force.

On receiving the order to take the Kremlin, I took a detachment of about 120 Zamoskvorechie Red Guards and 20 men from the 55th Regiment and moved with this detachment early in the morning on November 15th (2nd) onto Red Square, towards the Spassky Gate.

We went up to the gate and smashed it in. In reply machine gun fire was sprayed at us from the Kremlin bell towers, from Red Square, and from the roof of Commerce Row [now the GUM Department Store], fortunately badly aimed. Covered by the Kremlin wall, our detachment entered the courtyard. Right at the entrance to the gate we saw a mass of broken rifles, sabers, daggers, hand grenades, bombs, and shell casings. It was hard to move without stepping on a bomb or a shell casing. Our path was also obstructed by large piece of brick wall torn off by artillery fire, and piles of military supplies. Further on we had to move with great care in order not to fall into the shell holes. The cadets fought back. The cadets shooting at us were quickly joined by the cadets who had been hiding in the Nikolaevsky Palace, in spite of their declaration of surrender to the Military-Revolutionary Committee. So the Kremlin was taken by storm.

I remember one curious moment that struck us with its unexpectedness. Moving under the cover of the Kremlin buildings while rifle and machine gun fire was sprayed at us, we headed for the Nikolaevsky Palace. Suddenly from the chapel about forty priests and monks ran to meet us with ikons in their hands, crying "Brothers! Don't kill us!" I made them turn back, declaring, "We won't act as treacherously as you, and won't take revenge on prisoners. Tell your people, as soon as they give the word that they are surrendering they should promptly lay down their weapons."

They were offered five minutes to reply. Our ultimatum was complied with. In fact, after the five minutes officers, cadets, and students poured out of the Nikolaevsky Palace and the other buildings and came to meet us. Some of them committed suicide right then, others fell into a faint, still others like Colonel Pekarsky and his group came out seemingly without weapons but actually had hand grenades concealed on them.

Having beaten the cadets, we undertook right away to liberate our arrested comrades. The Red Guard detachment under the command of Comrade Petrov promptly freed the arrested soldiers of the 56th Regiment and our commander of the Kremlin arsenal, Comrade Berzin. Some of them were sick. However, in spite of their exhaustion and hunger, the liberated soldiers immediately grabbed rifles that had been thrown down by the cadets. It didn't go off without excesses: some of the liberated prisoners threw themselves at the colonel and the cadets who had shot their comrades and killed them on the spot. . . .

The Secret Police

With resistance to Soviet rule growing, the new government proceeded in December 1917 to establish the "Extraordinary Commission to Fight Counter-Revolution," or "Cheka," from its Russian initials. This agency, empowered to suppress all enemies of the regime, was the direct ancestor of the present KGB ("Committee of State Security"). It was authorized by the following Decree of the Council of People's Commissars, December 7, 1917. (Translated in Bunyan and Fisher, *The Bolshevik Revolution*, pp. 297–8.)

The Commission is to be named the All-Russian Extraordinary Commission and is to be attached to the Soviet of People's Commissars. [This commission] is to make war on counter-revolution and sabotage. . . .

The duties of the Commission will be:

1. To persecute and break up all acts of counter-revolution and sabotage all over Russia, no matter what their origin.

2. To bring before the Revolutionary Tribunal all counter-revolutionists and saboteurs and to work out a plan for fighting them.

3. To make preliminary investigation only—enough to break up [the counter-revolutionary act]. The Commission is to be divided into sections: (a) the information [section], (b) the organization section (in charge of organizing the fight against counter-revolution all over Russia) with branches, and (c) the fighting section.

The Commission will be formed tomorrow. . . . The Commission is to watch the press, saboteurs, strikers, and the Socialist-Revolutionists of the Right. Measures [to be taken against these counter-revolutionists are] confiscation, deprivation of [food] cards, publication of the names of the enemies of the people, etc.

The Dissolution of the Constituent Assembly

Following elections in November, 1917, in which the Bolsheviks ran a poor second to the SRs, the long-promised Constituent Assembly convened in the Tauride Palace (the old

Duma and Soviet building) in Petrograd. Following the election of the SR leader Victor Chernov as president of the Assembly, the Bolsheviks and Left SRs denounced the body as a counter-revolutionary vestige and walked out. At Lenin's initiative the Soviet Government decreed the Assembly dissolved, and troops closed it down the next day.

a) The brief proceedings and their rude termination were later described by the presiding officer, the SR Victor M. Chernov in "Russia's One-Day Parliament," *The New Leader,* January 31, 1948. (Copyright © 1948 by the American Labor Conference on International Affairs, Inc.; reprinted by permission).

When we, the newly elected members of the Constituent Assembly, entered the Tauride Palace, the seat of the Assembly in Petrograd, on January 18, 1918, we found that the corridors were full of armed guards. They were masters of the building, crude and brazen. At first they did not address us directly, and only exchanged casual observations to the effect that "this guy should get a bayonet between his ribs" or "it wouldn't be bad to put some lead into this one." When we entered the large hall, it was still empty. The Bolshevik deputies had not yet appeared.

A tank division billeted in Petrograd remained faithful to the Assembly. It intended to demonstrate this faithfulness by participating in the march to the Palace which was to pass on its way the barracks of the Preobrazhensky and Semenovsky Regiments, the two best units of the Petrograd garrison. At the meetings held by these regiments, resolutions were invariably adopted demanding the transfer of state power to the Constituent Assembly. Thus a prospect was open for the consolidation of democratic forces.

But the Bolsheviks were not caught off guard. They attacked the columns of demonstrators converging on the Tauride Palace from various parts of Petrograd. Whenever the unarmed crowd could not be dispersed immediately, the street was blocked by troops or Bolshevik units would shoot into the crowd. The demonstrators threw themselves on the pavement and waited until the rattle of machine guns quieted down; then they would jump up and continue their march, leaving behind the dead and wounded until they were stopped by a new volley. Or the crowd would be bayoneted by enraged Bolshevik outfits, which would get hold of the banners and placards carried by the demonstrators and tear them into scraps.

The Assembly hall was gradually filled by the deputies. Near the dais were placed armed guards. The public gallery was crowded to overflowing. Here and there glittered rifle muzzles. Admission tickets for the public were distributed by the notorious Uritsky. He did his job well. . . .

At last all the deputies had gathered in a tense atmosphere. The left sector was evidently waiting for something. From our benches rose Deputy Lordkipanidze, who said in a calm, businesslike voice that, according to an old parliamentary custom, the first sitting should be presided over by the senior deputy. The senior was S. P. Shvetsov, an old Socialist Revolutionary (SR).

As soon as Shvetsov's imposing figure appeared on the dais, somebody gave a signal, and a deafening uproar broke out. The stamping of feet, hammering on the desks and howling made an infernal noise. The public in the gallery and the Bolshevik allies, the Left Socialist Revolutionaries, joined in the tumult. The guards clapped their rifle butts on the floor. From various sides guns were trained on Shvetsov. He took the President's bell, but the tinkling was drowned in the noise. He put it back on the table, and somebody immediately grabbed it and handed it over, like a trophy, to the representative of the Sovnarkom [Council of People's Commissars], Sverdlov. Taking advantage of a moment of comparative silence, Shvetsov managed to pronounce the sacramental phrase: "The session of the Constituent Assembly is open." These words evoked a new din of protest. Shvetsov slowly left the dais and joined us. He was replaced by Sverdlov, who opened the session for the second time, but now in the name of the Soviets, and presented its "platform." This was an ultimatum: we had just to vote Aye or No.

In the election of the Assembly's President, the Bolsheviks presented no candidate of their own. They voted for Maria Spiridonova, nominated by the Left SRs. Later they threw Spiridonova into jail and tormented her until she was on the verge of insanity. But at this moment they wanted to take full advantage of her popularity and reputation as a martyr in the struggle against Tsarism. My nomination as candidate for the Presidency received even greater support than had been expected. Some leftist peasants evidently could not bring themselves to oppose their own "muzhik minister." I obtained 244 votes against 150.

I delivered my inauguration address, making vigorous efforts to keep self-control. Every sentence of my speech was met with outcries, some ironical, others spiteful, often buttressed by the brandishing of guns. Bolshevik deputies surged forward to the dais. Conscious that the stronger nerves would win, I was determined not to yield to provocation. I said that the nation had made its choice, that the composition of the Assembly was a living testimony to the people's yearning for Socialism, and that its convention marked the end of the hazy transition period. Land reform, I went on, was a foregone conclusion: the land would be equally accessible to all who wished to till it. The Assembly, I said, would inaugurate an era of active foreign policy directed toward peace.

I finished my speech amidst a cross-fire of interruptions and cries. It was now the turn of the Bolshevik speakers—Skvortsov and Bukharin. During their delivery, our sector was a model of restraint and self-discipline. We maintained a cold, dignified silence. The Bolshevik speeches, as usual, were shrill, clamorous, provocative and rude, but they could not break the icy silence of our majority. As President, I was bound in duty to call them to order for abusive statements. But I know that this was precisely what they expected. Since the armed guards were under their orders, they wanted clashes, incidents and perhaps a brawl. So I remained silent.

The Social Democratic Tseretelli rose to answer the Bolsheviks. They tried to "scare" him by levelling at him a rifle from the gallery and brandishing a gun in front of his face. I had to restore order—but how? Appeals to maintain the dignity of the Constituent Assembly evoked an even greater noise, at times turning into a raving fury. Dybenko and other demagogues called for more and more assaults. Lenin, in the government box, demonstrated his contempt for the Assembly by lounging in his chair and putting on the air of a man who was bored to death. I threatened to clear the gallery of the yelling public. Though this was an empty threat, since the guards were only waiting for the order to "clear" us out of the hall, it proved temporarily effective. Tseretelli's calm and dignified manner helped to restore peace.

There was a grim significance in the outburst that broke loose when a middle-of-the-road deputy, Severtsov-Odoyesky, started to speak Ukrainian. In the Assembly the Bolsheviks did not want to hear any language except Russian. I was compelled to state emphatically that in the new Russia, each nationality had the right to use its own language whenever it pleased.

When it appeared that we refused to vote the Soviet "platform" without discussion, the Bolsheviks walked out of the sitting in a body. They returned to read a declaration charging us with counter-revolution and stating that our fate would be decided by organs which were in charge of such things. Soon after that the Left SRs also made up their minds. Just before the discussion of the land reform started, their representative, I. Z. Steinberg, declared that they were in disagreement with the majority, and left the Assembly.

We knew that the Bolsheviks were in conference, discussing what to do next. I felt sure that we would be arrested. But it was of utmost importance for us to have a chance to say the last word. I declared that the next point on the agenda was the land reform. At this moment somebody pulled at my sleeve.

"You have to finish now. There are orders from the People's Commissar."

Behind me stood a stocky sailor, accompanied by his armed comrades.

"What People's Commissar?"

"We have orders. Anyway, you cannot stay here any longer. The lights will be turned out in a minute. And the guards are tired."

"The members of the Assembly are also tired but cannot rest until they have fulfilled the task entrusted to them by the people—to decide on the land reform and the future form of government."

And leaving the guards no time to collect themselves, I proceeded to read the main paragraphs of the Land Bill, which our party had prepared long ago. But time was running short. Reports and debates had to be omitted. Upon my proposal, the Assembly voted six basic points of the bill. It provided that all land was to be turned into common property, with every tiller possessing equal rights to use it. Amidst incessant shouts: "That's enough! Stop it now! Clear the hall!" the other points of the bill were voted.

Fearing that the lights would be extinguished, somebody managed to procure candles. It was essential that the future form of government be voted upon immediately. Otherwise the Bolsheviks would not fail to charge the Assembly with having left the door open for the restoration of the monarchy. The motion for a republican form of government was carried unanimously.

In the dawn of a foggy and murky morning I declared a recess until noon.

At the exit a palefaced man pushed his way to me and beseeched me in a trembling voice not to use my official car. A bunch of murderers, he said, was waiting for me. He admitted that he was a Bolshevik, but his conscience revolted against this plot.

I left the building, surrounded by a few friends. We saw several men in sailor's uniforms loitering near my car. We decided to walk. We had a long distance to go, and when I arrived home I learned that rumors were in circulation that the Constituent Assembly had dispersed, and that Chernov and Tseretelli had been shot.

At noon several members of the Assembly were sent on reconnaissance. They reported that the door of the Tauride Palace was sealed and guarded by a patrol with machine guns and two pieces of field artillery. Later in the day a decree of the Sovnarkom was published by which the Constituent Assembly was "dissolved."

Thus ended Russia's first and last democratic parliament.

b) The decree of dissolution referred to by Chernov was drafted by Lenin, who took this opportunity to affirm the principle of revolutionary dictatorship. The translated text is from Lenin, *Selected Works*, vol. 2, part 2, pp. 382–84. His action meant the end of any peaceful internal alternative to the political monopoly of the Bolshevik Party (soon to be renamed the Communist Party).

Draft Decree on the Dissolution of the Constituent Assembly

At its very inception, the Russian revolution gave rise to Soviets of Workers', Soldiers' and Peasants' Deputies as the only mass organization of all the toiling and exploited classes capable of leading the struggle of these classes for their complete political and economic emancipation.

During the whole of the initial period of the Russian revolution the Soviets multiplied in number, grew and gained strength, were taught by their own experience to discard the illusions of compromise with the bourgeoisie and to realize the deceptive nature of the forms of bourgeois-democratic parliamentarianism, and arrived by practical experience at the conclusion that the emancipation of the oppressed classes was impossible unless they broke with these forms and with every kind of compromise. Such a break was the October Revolution, which transferred the entire power to the Soviets.

The Constituent Assembly, elected on the basis of lists drawn up prior to the October Revolution, was an expression of the old relation of political forces which existed when power was held by the compromisers and the Kadets. When the people at that time voted for the candidates of the Socialist-Revolutionary Party, they were not in a position to choose between the Right Socialist-Revolutionaries, the supporters of the bourgeoisie, and the Left Socialist-Revolutionaries, the supporters of Socialism. Thus the Constituent Assembly, which was to have been the crown of the bourgeois parliamentary republic, could not but become an obstacle in the path of the October Revolution and the Soviet power.

The October Revolution, by giving the power to the Soviets, and through the Soviets to the toiling and exploited classes, aroused the desperate resistance of the exploiters, and in the crushing of this resistance it fully revealed itself as the beginning of the socialist revolution. The toiling classes learned by experience that the old bourgeois parliamentarism had outlived its purpose and was absolutely incompatible with the aim of achieving Socialism, and that not national institutions, but only class institutions (such as the Soviets), were capable of overcoming the resistance of the propertied classes and of laying the foundations of a socialist society. To relinquish the sovereign power of the Soviets, to relinquish the Soviet republic won by the people, for the sake of bourgeois parliamentarism and the Constituent Assembly, would now be a retrograde step and cause the collapse of the October workers' and peasants' revolution.

Owing to the circumstances mentioned above, the majority in the Constituent Assembly which met on January 5 was secured by the party of the Right Socialist-Revolutionaries, the party of Kerensky, Avksentyev and Chernov. Naturally, this party refused to discuss the absolutely clear, precise and unambiguous proposal of the supreme organ of Soviet power, the Central Executive Committee of the Soviets, to recognize the program of the Soviet power, to recognize the "Declaration of Rights of the Toiling and Exploited People," to recognize the October Revolution and the Soviet power. Thereby the Constituent Assembly severed all ties with the Soviet Republic of Russia. The withdrawal from such a Constituent Assembly of the groups of the Bolsheviks and the Left Socialist-Revolutionaries, who now patently constitute the overwhelming majority in the Soviets and enjoy the confidence of the workers and the majority of the peasants, was inevitable.

The Right Socialist-Revolutionary and Menshevik parties are in fact waging outside the walls of the Constituent Assembly a most desperate struggle against the Soviet power, calling openly in their press for its overthrow and characterizing as arbitrary and unlawful the crushing by force of the resistance of the exploiters by the toiling classes, which is essential in the interests of emancipation from exploitation. They are defending the saboteurs, the servitors of capital, and are going to the length of undisguised calls to terrorism, which certain "unidentified groups" have already begun to practice. It is obvious that under such circumstances the remaining part of the Constituent Assembly could only serve as a screen for the struggle of the counterrevolutionaries to overthrow the Soviet power.

Accordingly, the Central Executive Committee resolves:

The Constituent Assembly is hereby dissolved.

Further Readings

The standard general account of the Russian Revolution is still William Henry Chamberlin, *The Russian Revolution,* 2 vols. (New York: Macmillan, 1935). E. H. Carr's monumental *History of Soviet Russia* (London and New York: Macmillan, 1950–   ) devotes three volumes to the Revolution (mainly post-October). Marcel Leibman, *The Russian Revolution* (New York: Random House, 1970) is a good one-volume account by a Belgian scholar. Alan Moorehead's *The Russian Revolution* (New York: Harper, 1958) is slightly sensationalist. Richard Pipes, ed., *Revolutionary Russia* (Cambridge, Mass.: Harvard University Press, 1968) is an interesting collection of scholarly essays. The Soviet view is available in translation in P. N. Sobolev, *et al.,* eds., *History of the October Revolution* (Moscow: Progress Publishers, 1966).

The memoir-histories are a multitude. In addition to those by Francis, Miliukov, Kerensky, Sukhanov, Chernov, and Trotsky represented in this book, the reader may consult Raphael R. Abramovich, *The Soviet Revolution* (New York: International Universities Press, 1962)—a Menshevik view; Sir George Buchanan (the British Ambassador), *My Mission to Russia & Other Diplomatic Memories* (Boston: Little, Brown, 1923); Kerensky, *Russia and History's Turning Point* (New York: Duell, Sloan & Pierce, 1965); R. A. Bruce Lockhart, *British Agent* (New York: Putnam's, 1933); John Reed, *Ten Days That Shook The World* (New York: Boni & Liveright, 1918); Victor Shklovsky, *A Sentimental Journey: Memoirs, 1917–1922* (Ithaca, N.Y.: Cornell University Press, 1970); W. S. Voytinsky, *Stormy Passage* (New York: Vanguard, 1961); Albert Rhys Williams, *Through The Russian Revolution* (1921; reissued, New York: Monthly Review Press, 1967).

Important histories of particular periods of the Revolution include Sir Bernard Pares, *The Fall of the Russian Monarchy* (New York: Knopf, 1939); George Katkov, *Russia, 1917: The February Revolution* (London: Longmans, 1967); Marc Ferro, *La Revolution de 1917 (February–July),* (Paris: Aubier, 1967); Alexander Rabinowitch, *Prelude to Revolution: The Petrograd Bolsheviks & the July 1917 Uprising* (Bloomington, Ind.: Indiana University Press, 1968); Oliver Radkey, *The Agrarian Foes of Bolshevism: Promise*

& *Default of the Russian Socialist Revolutionaries, February to October, 1917* (New York: Columbia University Press, 1958); Robert V. Daniels, *Red October: The Bolshevik Revolution of 1917* (New York: Scribner's, 1967).

Outstanding biographies of the leading revolutionary figures include Adam Ulam, *The Bolsheviks* (on Lenin), (New York: Macmillan, 1965); Isaac Deutscher, *The Prophet Armed: Trotsky 1879–1921* (New York: Oxford University Press, 1954); and Deutscher, *Stalin: A Political Biography* (New York & London: Oxford University Press, 1949). For biographical and autobiographical sketches of the lesser Bolshevik figures see Georges Haupt and Jean-Jacques Marie, *Les Bolchéviks par eux-mêmes* (Paris: Maspero, 1969).

There are several useful anthologies of historical commentary and memoir material, including Arthur E. Adams, *The Russian Revolution and Bolshevik Victory: Why and How?* (Boston: Heath, 1960); M. K. Dziewanowski, *The Russian Revolution: An Anthology* (New York: Crowell, 1970); Robert H. McNeal, *The Russian Revolution: Why Did The Bolsheviks Win?* (New York: Holt, Rinehart & Winston, 1959); Dmitri von Mohrenschildt, *The Russian Revolution of 1917: Contemporary Accounts* (New York: Oxford Univ. Press, 1971); Roger Pethybridge, *Witness to the Russian Revolution* (London: Allen & Unwin, 1965). The major collections of documents in translation—by Browder & Kerensky, Bunyan & Fisher, and Golder—have been drawn from in this book. Of special additional interest is Z. A. B. Zeman, *Germany and the Revolution in Russia, 1915–1918: Documents from the Archives of the German Foreign Ministry* (New York: Oxford University Press, 1958).

Essays on the historiography of the Russian Revolution include Michael Karpovich, "The Russian Revolution of 1917," *Journal of Modern History,* vol. 2, 1930, pp. 258–80; James H. Billington, "Six Views of the Russian Revolution," *World Politics,* April, 1966; and David Anin, "The February Revolution: Was the Collapse Inevitable," *Soviet Studies,* April, 1967. On Soviet work see Robert V. Daniels, "Soviet Historians Prepare for the Fiftieth," *Slavic Review,* March, 1967.

DATE DUE